Joseph B Stratton

Following Christ, a Manual for Church-Members

Joseph B Stratton

Following Christ, a Manual for Church-Members

ISBN/EAN: 9783743305861

Manufactured in Europe, USA, Canada, Australia, Japa

Cover: Foto ©ninafisch / pixelio.de

Manufactured and distributed by brebook publishing software (www.brebook.com)

Joseph B Stratton

Following Christ, a Manual for Church-Members

CONTENTS.

CHAPTER I.
INTRODUCTORY	7

CHAPTER II.
TRUE CONCEPTION OF RELIGIOUS LIVING 14

CHAPTER III.
RULE OF RELIGIOUS LIVING 39

CHAPTER IV.
OBSERVANCE OF PUBLIC WORSHIP 75

CHAPTER V.
PRIVATE PRAYER 93

CHAPTER VI.
THE CULTIVATION OF PERSONAL RELIGION 115

CHAPTER VII.
RELIGION IN THE CHURCH 135

CHAPTER VIII.

Religion in Secular Life 156

CHAPTER IX.

Religion in the Family 187

CHAPTER X.

Religion Always and Everywhere 213

CHAPTER XI.

Conclusion 231

FOLLOWING CHRIST.

CHAPTER I.

INTRODUCTORY.

AS the Scriptures employ the phrase "confessing Christ" to describe the assuming of a religious character and life, they very naturally employ the corresponding phrase "following Christ" to describe the exhibition of such a character and the prosecution of such a life. In adopting religion under the direction of the Bible, a man attaches himself to Christ; in practicing religion under the same direction, he follows Christ. We may be thankful that a procedure so critical in its nature, and so momentous in its bearings and issues as this latter one must needs be, has been set before us by God in terms so simple and intelligible. Jesus constructed no formal system of doctrine and enacted no formal code of moral law, but he comprehended both in the injunction "Follow me." Light sufficient for the world is concentrated in this single luminous point.

Every honest person, in embracing a religious character and life, will desire above all things to know what is precisely included in the great obligation he has assumed. He will desire this for two reasons: *first*, that he may be sure that nothing properly belonging to its contents has been overlooked; and *second*, that he may be sure, at the same time, that nothing apart from or beyond those contents has been imposed upon him. The position of one who by proper acknowledgments before the authorities of the church, and by a participation in the covenanting ordinances of baptism and the Lord's Supper, has just taken the step which attests the faith and avows the purpose of a Christian, must be an unspeakably solemn one to the party concerned; and one which every thoughtful observer will look upon with the profoundest interest and the tenderest solicitude. If it means what it ought to mean, it presents us with that spectacle of a sinner repenting and turning from his evil ways over which the angels of God rejoice in heaven. It is the return to the Father's house of a wandering prodigal to whom every right-minded "elder son" will be ready to extend a loving welcome. It is the enlistment of a new recruit in the army of Christ—an act which surely should appeal with a pathetic power to the heart of every veteran in that army.

Young soldier, you have done a brave deed—a deed which many a man who has courage enough to face death on the battlefield does not dare to do. You have dared to confess that your life heretofore has been all wrong, and to determine that in future it shall by God's help be made right. You have dared to change masters, to change principles, to change habits. You have rescued yourself from the thraldom of sin; you have broken loose from the appetites with which it had enslaved you and the associations with which it had entangled you. You have renounced all other lords which have had dominion over you to bow the knee to Jesus.

The struggle by which you have done all this may have been great; the severity of it reveals itself in the sobriety of your manner and the seriousness of your countenance. A deeper shade still gathers over your spirit as you think of the struggles to come—as you contemplate the responsibilities which are involved in the steps which yet lie before you. The apprehension of failure or of defection in the work you have undertaken fills you with alarm. Shall the peace, the hope, the joy, of a new life which are now stirring in your soul be stifled and lost? Shall the Lord ever have occasion to look upon you as he did upon Peter, and reproach you for your unfaithfulness and treachery? Shall the friends in Christ to whom you have now joined yourself be constrained in time to come to mourn over your backsliding? And shall the unbelieving crowd whom you have professedly abandoned have cause to rejoice over your halting?

To all such questions you now make the

almost passionate reply, "God forbid!" The very gravity of your demeanor, the intensity of desire and purpose which kindles the very look of your eye, seem to make a mute appeal to others more advanced in Christian life to instruct your ignorance and brace up your feebleness— to tell you, in a word, what you must be and what you must do in order to realize the character you have assumed and the life you have undertaken to enact.

In the spirit of sympathy with this mute appeal (which in many instances has been addressed to the writer as a spoken one) the following pages have been prepared. In the preparation of them the keynote with which everything will be kept in harmony is the great comprehensive command, the first (Matt. iv. 19) and the last (John xxi. 22) addressed by Christ to his disciples, "Follow me." It is evidently enough for the disciple that he be "as his Master," and for the servant that he be "as his Lord" (Matt. x. 25). The religion of Christianity requires just this likeness to Christ—all this, and nothing more than this.

The exposition of this cardinal law of the Christian life, it is hoped, will furnish a seasonable aid to that favored class of persons who through God's blessing upon faithful parental training have by imperceptible steps been brought into his kingdom. Divine grace, in the nature of it, is without limitation as to the time and manner of its operation. It is the privilege of all who are themselves in covenant with God to believe that their offspring may be included with them in the provisions of the covenant. They often give evidence that they are. In such cases the birth of the Spirit has supervened upon the birth of the flesh at so early a day, and by such insensible processes, that the subject has no consciousness of the regenerating change. But the obligations of the Christian life are the same in the case of those who are thus called from the womb as in that of those who are converted in later life. The import of these obligations will present itself to the intelligence of these persons, as well as of others, when the time arrives for them to avow their faith in Christ and their consecration to God by a formal union with the Church. To them, as well as to others who have been recalled from the open paths of unbelief and sin, Jesus says, "Follow me." The counsels which befit the latter class may be as diligently studied and as carefully observed by them. The Spirit of Christ in the soul of a believer will manifest its presence by the same phenomena in the case of a Samuel sanctified from his birth as in that of a Saul arrested by sovereign grace in a career of flagrant opposition to Christ.

CHAPTER II.

THE TRUE CONCEPTION OF RELIGIOUS LIVING.

THE sincere professor of the religion of Christ will mean something very definite by the profession which he has made. If in all enterprises it is requisite that a man should have 'a clear idea of what he is doing, it is especially requisite in the practice of religion, confessedly the most important enterprise in which man can engage. No one has ever risen to the grandeur of a Christian life who has not felt the necessity of intelligently and deliberately weighing and measuring the import of such a life.

"Which of you" asks the Saviour (Luke xiv. 28), "intending to build a tower, sitteth not down first and counteth the cost, whether he have sufficient to finish it? Lest haply, after he hath laid the foundation and is not able to finish it, all that behold it begin to mock him, saying, This man began to build, and was not able to finish. Or what king, going to make war with another king, sitteth not down first and consulteth whether he be able with ten thousand to meet him that cometh against him with twenty thousand?" With the breadth and the closeness of circumspection indicated by these operations the young Christian ought to scrutinize the nature, the scope and the aim of the movement in which he is embarking.

Who would start upon a journey without having a destination in view, or without endeavoring to foresee and provide for all the conditions necessary for a sure and safe transit to the desired point, and for the attainment of the objects proposed in the purpose to visit it?

A recent traveler, in a work describing a tour around the world, tells us that "he had planned his entire excursion several months before setting out, with the times of arrival and departure for each country that he expected to visit; and until reaching Europe, where his plans were intentionally left uncertain, he was scarcely a day out of time at any stage of the journey." Of course such a journey was wisely and successfully made; the traveler accomplished just what he intended to do. The traveler upon the Christian life can hope for a satisfactory issue to his undertaking only by exercising the same forethought. Standing within the threshold of the Church, with a future consecrated to Christ before him, the earnest inquiry of his soul ought to be, and will be if he is a true man, "Lord, what wilt thou have me to do?"

That there are deliberate dissemblers and hypocrites in the Church is undoubtedly true, but such cases are extremely rare. Ordinarily, those who formally make a profession of religion are sincere. It may happen that the act has been performed under an emotional excitement, and that after the transient inspiration has subsided the individual has relapsed into his old form of life, but still he was sincere when the profession was made. He was deceived in persuading himself that he was a subject of regenerating grace, but he was honest in entertaining the persuasion. Simon Magus even (Acts viii. 13) gives evidence of being honest when he professed faith and received baptism as a disciple of Jesus, though he afterward showed that his "heart was not right in the sight of God."

If the genuine principle of spiritual life is in the newly-enlisted church-member, he will be honest not only in the persuasion that he is a Christian, but in the sense of desiring to know and meaning to be and to do all that is implied in the name and character of a Christian. *Whither this journey upon which he has entered is to lead him, and what is involved in the prosecution of it*, are the anxious and absorbing inquiries which his mind will be constrained to revolve. On these inquiries a few reflections which I shall proceed to offer may throw light.

I.

It is evident that the idea of religious living, as given in the phrase "Following

Christ," includes vastly more than a mere external religiousness or the putting on of a religious manner and the practicing of a certain set of religious acts and rites.

A religion of the look, the tone, the dress, the outward ceremonial, has received the distinctive name of "sanctimoniousness"—an opprobrious term by which the world has denounced a religion of form and appearance as a spurious religion. Real religion is a property of the man himself. It is not made by the drapery he wears, or the dialect he uses, or the society to which he attaches himself. The follower of Christ will change his ways *because he is* a Christian, not in order to become a Christian.

Even under the Old Dispensation, where external signs of membership in the Church were so largely enjoined, the principle was distinctly announced (1 Sam. xvi. 7): "The Lord seeth not as man seeth; for man looketh on the outward appearance, but the Lord looketh on the heart." No right-minded professor of religion will delude himself with the idea that his vow of discipleship is fulfilled by the putting on of a religious demeanor or the doing merely the things which religious people ordinarily do. He will feel that he meant vastly more than pledging himself to appear in the house of God on the Sabbath, to repeat two or three prayers a day, to come to the communion-table at the stated times, to subscribe for a missionary paper, to drop his contribution into the collection-box and to vote at a church-meeting, when he pledged himself to follow Christ. He will know that there is no "keeping of the words" of Christ without "loving" Christ (John xiv. 23), and love puts the consecration of the heart at the root of acts of devotion.

Religion, it is true, like every other strong spiritual force introduced into a man, may be expected to impress itself more or less upon his manner and conduct. In some instances it may effect a total transformation of character, as in the case of St. Paul, changing the lion into the lamb. It certainly will make the man who has been neglectful of religious customs and observances attentive to them; it will manifest its presence in the soul by this outward sign. But a sign is not identical with the thing it represents; the fruit of a tree is not the tree nor the life of the tree.

There may be the sign of religion where there is no religion. The Jews in Isaiah's time (Isa. i.) were scrupulous in keeping their festivals, bringing their oblations and offering up their prayers, and yet in the sight of God there was "no soundness in them." The Pharisees in our Saviour's time made themselves conspicuous by their badges of piety, but were likened by him to "whited sepulchres." The mere calling Christ "Lord, Lord," or the acknowledging him by any other symbolical act, does not make a man a member of the kingdom of heaven (Matt. vii. 21.) The honest soldier of Christ, in espousing a religious life, will not mistake the wearing of a church uniform or the practicing of a church drill for such a life. It is not the new garb, but the new heart—not the form of godliness, but the spirit of it—which is required for the following of Jesus.

II.

Nor is the act of entering into church-membership to be regarded as a mere induction into a corporation and a subscription to the laws of that corporation.

Men have found it convenient or necessary in the prosecution of a variety of objects to unite themselves under a social compact or constitution; they thus form a league or confederation for a special purpose. There must be, of course, in every such league or confederation, a set of laws bearing upon the object proposed by it, by which every person entering it is bound. By this his duty as a member of it is limited and defined. A temperance society, for instance, adopts its rules with a view to the promotion of temperance, and he who joins it engages to observe these rules. So long as this is done all is done that is required of him. To put the church in the same category with a temperance society, and to construe the phrase "joining the church" as signifying the same kind of act as the joining of such a society, is a fundamental mistake. In becoming a church-member a man is, indeed, entering a social body and placing himself, to a certain extent, under the obligations involved in the constitution of that body. The church is the house of God, and, like every other house, it must have its peculiar economy—that is, its *house-law*. This house-law, which sets certain objects before the church and prescribes certain rules and methods for the attainment of them, requires organization and concerted effort on the part of the members. The worship of God, for instance, is to be maintained in the world, and this creates a necessity for a number of practical arrangements involving an exercise of deliberation and an expenditure of money in which every member must share. It is his duty in his measure to do whatever the church as a body is required to do, and a duty which he owes to the body; so that his fellow-members are wronged whenever he fails to do it.

But no intelligent disciple of Christ would for a moment substitute compliance with this house-law of the church for obedience to the law of God, or feel that in discharging his duty to the corporation of which he was a member he had acquitted himself of his obligations as a follower of Christ. His social life as a church-member is only one department—and a lower one —of that religious life which he is bound to lead as a Christian ; and if his aim is only to do the will of his brethren, he has failed to recognize the first principle of religious living, which is to do the will of his Father in heaven. To stand well and to have a fair report among those with whom he has associated himself in church-fellowship is an end which every professor of religion ought to keep in view ; but if his purpose contemplates no higher end than this, it will certainly never realize itself in making him a follower of Christ.

III.

As mere conformity to church-regulations is not the rule of religious living, neither is union with the church to be made the ground upon which the Christian rests his expectation of spiritual blessings.

The church cannot do the work of Christ; it cannot regenerate nor sanctify nor save. It is not a divinely-instituted insurance-company, pledging itself, in consideration of their compliance with certain terms of membership, to protect its subscribers from all spiritual loss and damage. Under some theories, conspicuously the Romish, this idea is unquestionably the cardinal one. The Church is represented as a mother, assuming the custody and guaranteeing the salvation of all who put themselves under her charge. It is held forth as an asylum within whose sacred enclosure the inmate will be shielded from the pursuit of law and furnished with all the aids of grace. Let the church-member, it is said, implicitly accept the teachings of the Church and regularly comply with its ordinances, and the Church pledges to him an assured interest in all the privileges of the kingdom of heaven.

This is simply a modification of the old Jewish doctrine which identified religion with relationship to Abraham—a doctrine which John the Baptist denounced when he cried (Matt. iii. 9), "Think not to say within yourselves, We have Abraham to our father, for I say unto you that God is able of these stones to raise up children unto Abraham;" and which the Saviour condemned when he said (Matt. viii. 11), "Many shall come from the east and the west, and sit down with Abraham and Isaac and Jacob in the kingdom of heaven; but the children of the kingdom shall be cast out into outer darkness." It is the prerogative of Christ personally to forgive sin, to reconcile the soul to God and to bestow eternal life; and he has never delegated this prerogative to his Church, and no policy or certificate that church authorities can issue is of any worth unless Christ has first pronounced the believer forgiven and justified. The man who puts dependence upon a Church in the place of following Christ is indulging a fatal delusion.

IV.

In distinction from these low and superficial views of a religious life the Bible places the foundation and source of it in a new nature. It represents the Christian, not as an old creature rehabilitated and newly shaped and labeled, but as a new creature specifically, one quickened by a new principle and reanimated and energized by a new spirit (2 Cor. v. 17. Rom. viii. 9).

The term "religious living" simply means the religious man living. If the church-member in entering upon a course of religious living has made a change in his mode of living, it is because he has himself undergone a change of nature, or what our Lord calls (John iii. 3) a new birth. The change in the outward and demonstrative is merely the sequel of a change which has occurred within him. By this change the carnal mind by which he was previously governed has given place, through faith in Christ, to a spiritual mind; love to God has been elevated above love to the creature, and all the minor affections are embraced and controlled by this predominant one. The law by which the believer's living is now directed and ordered requires him to be religious and forbids him to be anything else. "How shall we that are dead to sin," asks St. Paul (Rom. vi. 2), "live any longer therein?" How can the man in whose nature love to God has been implanted as the reigning principle be anything but a religious man in his living? As well might we ask, "How can the star be a star without shining?" or, "How can a fruit tree be a fruit tree without bearing fruit?"

Religious living is expressed not so much by the phrase "I do" as by the phrase "I am;" consequently, in making a profession of religion the man is making a promise, not to do certain specified things, but *to be* in all things a certain definite character. He purposes and he pledges himself to be at all times and in all circumstances a Christian man. In private as well as in public, in secular transactions as well as sacred ones, on weekdays as well as on the Sabbath, outside of the church as well as in it, he recognizes the obligation as resting upon him to exhibit the nature of one born of God.

V.

A Christian life, conducted under the promptings of this new nature, will express itself actively in a species of working corresponding to this nature.

Every honest professor of religion will feel that he has bound himself by a solemn indenture to be a worker for God. It is only under this form that his living can claim to be a following of Christ, for Christ affirms of himself (John vi. 38), "I came down from heaven, not to do mine own will, but the will of him that sent me." Put the term "business" here in this passage in the place of the term "will," as we may properly do, and it will teach that in the believer's scheme of life God's business must take precedence of his own.

The privileges of the gospel can never be divorced from the duties of the gospel. The faith that receives Christ as a Saviour will receive him also as a Master. "Freely ye have received," as a statement of gratuitous blessings conferred, must always stand conjoined in the policy of the Christian with the injunction "Freely give." We are engrafted into Christ by the divine Husbandman not merely that we may live, but that we may give evidence of our living by our acting or working. "Herein is my Father glorified," says the Lord (John xv. 8), "that ye bear much fruit; so shall ye be my disciples."

The "high calling" which every follower of Jesus has received binds him to make the glory of God the chief end of his living. He is the servant entrusted with special talents by his Lord, and the command "Occupy"—trade with these—"till I come" accompanies the trust. "Always abounding in the work of the Lord" is a definition of, as well as a precept to, the Christian. He is to "work out his own salvation," or to prove himself to be in a state of salvation by his working. He is to "minister," as his Master did, to the good of others. He is to show his love to God by his love to his brethren. He is to pray for the coming of the kingdom of God, and to show that his praying is sincere by working for the coming of that kingdom. He is to make his light so positively and conspicuously shine that all in the house may see it. He is to travel with hourly diligence and with lifelong effort to the promised land, not be borne there in his luxurious car without a care or a movement of his own.

The relation of all other avocations to the supreme one of working for Christ is well stated by an eminent living minister in the pithy questions, "Is religion your business, or business your religion? Does your candle shine upon the bushel, or does the bushel hide your candle?" When Christ gives the command "Follow me," he imposes an obligation which involves in it the forsaking of all for his sake. Henceforth the business of God outranks and holds in subordination to itself all other exercises of life in the believer.

VI.

Religious living, furthermore, is to be conceived of as the carrying out of the engagements of a covenant between the soul and God.

Whatever may be the form of the process, no man becomes a Christian man without making a covenant with God. It may be expressed in literal terms. Dr. Doddridge has inserted such a covenant in his *Rise and Progress of Religion in the Soul* for the use of persons adopting a religious life. If this is not done literally, it is done virtually, by every one who embraces such a life.

The form of this covenant in Old-Testament times is stated by Isaiah (xxiii. 13): "O Lord our God, other lords beside thee have had dominion over us; but by thee only will we make mention of thy name." An example of it is given in Josh. xxiv. 22–26. After drawing from the people a profession of their allegiance to God, Joshua seals, as it were, the covenant into which they had entered by setting up a great stone under an oak that was near the sanctuary of the Lord and saying to the people, "Behold, this stone shall be a witness unto us, for it hath heard all the words of the Lord which he spake unto us; it shall be, therefore, a witness unto you, lest ye deny your God."

In the New Testament this covenant is described or suggested in various forms, as in these passages: "Ye also are become dead to the law by the body of Christ, that ye should be married to another, even to him who is raised from the dead, that we should bring forth fruit unto God" (Rom. vii. 4); "Ye who were without Christ, being aliens from the commonwealth of Israel and strangers from the covenant of promise, having no hope and without God in the world, now, in Christ Jesus, are made nigh by the blood of Christ" (Eph. ii. 12, 13); and "I have espoused you to one husband, that I may present you as a chaste virgin to Christ" (2 Cor. xi. 2).

Baptism and the Lord's Supper are essentially covenanting transactions. They are modes by which faith in Christ as the Prophet, the Priest and the King of the people of God is professed by the party engaging in them. If they mean anything, they mean that that party is by these solemn rites binding himself to make Christ in fact his Prophet, his Priest and his King. And these ordinances, being direct and positive institutions of God, have in them all the significance of a pledge or a seal on God's part that the blessings secured by the threefold work of Christ shall be conferred upon him.

All covenanting is a serious procedure, but in covenanting with God the procedure reaches a climax in both force and extent. The man's true self and his whole self must be conveyed to God in it; all other interests and obligations must be covered by it. All the countless circles through which life revolves—personal, domestic, political—must be included in and bounded by that supreme one which passes between the soul and God.

VII.

As a consequence of this last fact, Christian living is to be conceived of as the carrying out of a vow of consecration to God.

If it be a following of Christ, it must have a constant reference to the redemption of Christ as the source of both its motive and its rule. Now, an act, a life, of self-devotement on his part is clearly the only proportionate acknowledgment which the believer can make to that unspeakable demonstration of his love to him which God has made in the gospel. It is the response on man's side—and the only one possible—which corresponds with the call addressed to him on God's side. As every Christian has been bought with a price, even "the precious blood of Christ" (1 Pet. i. 19), he is no longer his own, but belongs to Him who died for him and rose again. A child of wrath by nature, even as others, he has become in Christ a child of God. As such he must yield himself in all respects to the demands of this sacred relationship. As such he must freely assent to the absolute claim which God has to the service of his life. He must present himself, soul, body and spirit, as a living sacrifice to him. He must regard himself as charged with a "holy priesthood," and as such separated to the work of showing forth the praises of Him who has called him unto his kingdom and glory.

When Christ prayed for the disciples (John xvii. 17) that they might be "sanctified" through the truth, he prayed that they might be so consecrated to a priestly life. As for their sakes he had so sanctified himself, or devoted himself to the doing of the Father's will, so he invoked upon them the grace which should enable them, as his followers, to realize the same consecrated spirit.

The apostles continually press the same idea upon their readers as the cardinal principle of Christian piety, as in those impassioned appeals of St. Paul to the Corinthians (2 Cor. vi. 14–18): "What fellowship hath righteousness with unrighteousness? And what communion hath light with darkness? And what concord hath Christ with Belial? Or what part hath he that believeth with an infidel? And what agreement hath the temple of God with idols? For ye are the temple of the living God; as God hath said, I will dwell in them and walk in them; and I will be their God, and they shall be my people. Wherefore come out from among them, and be ye separate, saith the Lord, and touch not the unclean thing; and I will receive you and will be a Father unto you, and you shall be my sons and daughters, saith the Lord Almighty."

The honest professor of religion will understand the thoroughness of the self-devotement involved in the act of profession. He will forsake all to follow Christ, and in the surrender will make no reserve —will keep back no part of the price.

VIII.

These views of the Christian life, deep and far-reaching as they are, certainly correspond with the form of that life presented in the Scriptures. They must be true if the Christian religion has anything of the significance ascribed to it by the inspired writers.

It cannot be safe to reject them as extravagant or fanatical, for that would be to charge the Saviour and his apostles with misleading and trifling with the souls they are evidently so anxious to guide into the way of life. It cannot be safe to follow the lower standards of religious living which may be common among professed Christians, for that would be to put the human idea of religion in the place of the divine.

O believer, see to it that these views are well weighed and deliberately accepted in making your profession of religion! Mistakes in your negotiations with God must be fatal to the whole transaction. Fair-dealing is the only kind of dealing which can have success with him, and fair-dealing here requires that your true self, and your whole self, should be given to him when you profess to become his servant.

Remember, it is your soul which you are seeking to save, your soul which Christ died to redeem, your soul which the Holy Spirit is employed in sanctifying. It is with the soul that you must realize and express your religion. Unless the soul has been united to Christ, there is no life in you; unless the soul has uttered itself in your vows of church-membership, they have been an empty form; unless the soul has gone with your sacramental acts, there is no meaning in them. It would have been better if they had never been performed, for they have been but a semblance and a pretence. Your religious life, if such it can be called, will be a heartless and mechanical servitude without consistency or effectiveness, without value in the sight of God and without comfort to yourself. To enter the church with any other views than those which have been described will be to entail upon you the misery of attempting to serve two masters, will expose you to endless self-contradictions, and will leave you, like the branch that abideth not in the vine, to be ultimately withered, cast out and burned in the fire.

CHAPTER III.

THE RULE OF RELIGIOUS LIVING.

A RELIGIOUS life is one which at all points maintains a contact and a communication with God.

That "God is not in all his thoughts" (Ps. x. 4) is the definition of an irreligious man. The reverse is true of the religious man: God is in all his thoughts; the law of the Lord is his meditation day and night. The motive, the purpose, the act, which is not coupled with faith in God and does not recognize his authority, however good and commendable it may be under certain aspects, is not religious. Every step in religious living must be taken, so to speak, in company with God, and must help to form a walk with God. Following Christ is at the same time a "walking in him" (Col. ii. 6).

It is of the first importance to the Christian—indeed, it is the very condition of his spiritual health and progress—that he should be kept consciously and intelligently under the influence of this association with God in Christ. Hence, in seeking for a rule for his religious life he must assure himself that everything which it contains expresses the mind of God and is accompanied by the authority of God.

The conscience is enfeebled and vitiated just in proportion as it admits the right of any other sovereign to control it. The religious affections become morbid and fantastic whenever they are stimulated by merely human excitements or directed through merely human channels. The proper vital element of the soul is the "inspiration of the Almighty." The inspiration of man is a source of disease and corruption, just as the body is sustained by the pure atmospheric air breathed down upon it from the regions above, and sickens when exposed to the mephitic gases which spring from the earth beneath. To usurp the prerogative of God and arbitrarily to burden the consciences of men with a schedule of duties of its own invention, as the Romish Church has done, is to bring the minds of its subjects into the grossest bondage and to expose them to the vagaries of a blind superstition. To teach, for instance, that holiness, which is the essential attribute of God, and which attaches only to things which he has seen fit to associate with himself, is attached to places and times and relics, is to break the bond of faith by which the soul is kept in union with God and to make it the victim of an indefinite credulity. From such a debasing apostasy as this Christ came to deliver his followers, and therefore he taught them that the true worshipers of God are those who worship him, not by frequenting certain shrines or observing certain rites, but "in spirit and in truth;" and that the keeping of the traditions of men is practically a rejecting of the commandments of God (Mark vii. 9).

I.

It is clear, therefore, that the Christian is to seek his great rule of living in the

Bible. From the character which is assumed by that book as the "word of God" and the "law of the Lord," it exactly fills the place which is required of anything which claims to be a rule of religious living, and a place which nothing else claiming to be such a rule can fill. Whatever the Bible enjoins as right or forbids as wrong is presented to the believer as right or wrong in the judgment of God; he accepts it as right or wrong on the direct ground of God's authority. This authority is legitimate; in acknowledging it the soul is acting both rationally and religiously.

The adequacy of the Bible as a rule of life is also complete. It is one of the strongest proofs that it is the product of a divine Mind that it is so constructed as to meet all the requirements of a directory for all men in following Christ. It accomplishes its objects in a manner which is thorough and peculiar to itself. It does not propound a code of formal laws prescribing by what particular acts a man is to serve God or by what set of doings or not-doings he is to prove himself a Christian man. From the outset it draws a distinction between "the letter" and "the spirit." It acts upon the principle that you must make the tree good before you can expect the fruit to be good. If it writes the ten commandments on visible tablets of stone, it shows that they all hang upon the law, "Thou shalt love the Lord thy God, with all thy heart, and with all thy soul, and with all thy mind" (Matt. xxii. 37). It begins its work of regulating the life of the man by regulating the affections and dispositions that lie within him, so that his supreme desire shall be to do the will of his Father in heaven. It purges the eye of the traveler before it sets before him the map from which he is to learn his way. As the Saviour teaches (John vii. 17), it is the man who "wills"—that is, *wishes*—to do God's will to whom the doctrine, the positive law, of God becomes intelligible and authoritative.

The Bible next to such a willing mind communicates such a conception of the character and mind of God as makes it easy for the believer to determine in all cases and at all seasons what his will must be. The Bible is from first to last a revelation of God. The faithful student of it grows in the knowledge of God from day to day; and, as God is the embodiment of all the elements and principles of rectitude, the knowledge of him is identical with a knowledge of these elements and principles. In the light of them the honest seeker can always find the path of duty. He does not need, like the man walking through the intricate streets of a city by night, to track his way by the blaze of a series of lamps, but it lies before him clearly defined in the broad sunlight by which the whole scene around him is illumined.

Once more, the Bible does its work by keeping the mind of the follower of Christ always directly under the wholesome influence of God's immediate presence and guidance. As it is the attractive property of the magnet which keeps the needle pointing to it, so the soul, under the impressions communicated to it by God's word, is pervaded with a spiritual susceptibility or tractability of temper toward God which makes it almost spontaneously respond to every intimation of his will. Thus Jesus says (John vi. 44) that it is through a "drawing" of the Father that any man comes to him. It is this habitual or instinctive cleaving of the soul to God—this "following hard after him," as the Psalmist calls it (Ps. lxiii. 8)—which keeps the Christian in the right ways of God and protects him from converting religious living into a mere self-imposed will-worship on the one hand, or a mere mechanical ritualism on the other.

To the question, therefore, "By what rule am I to regulate my conduct?" which the professor of religion will naturally ask, and ought to ask, I would answer, The Bible. Take that as the "man of your counsel," and use other guides only as aids to your knowledge of that. The Bible, if studied with the simple desire to know the will of God and with a fair and intelligent application of its teachings, will give you all the light you need. Whatever formal rules you may see fit to adopt must be drawn from this source, or they can have no authority over you. By going to the original fountain you will be kept most sensibly under the very law of God, and, furthermore, will be sufficiently thrown upon your own vigilance and discretion to keep your sense of responsibility for the manner of your living in habitual and healthy exercise.

Be, then, above all things, if you wish to be a genuine follower of Christ, a student of the Bible. And by the term "student" here I mean much more than a mere reader. The distinction between these terms I shall endeavor to point out in the following remarks.

II.

In order to study the Bible, it must be read with a purpose or for the sake of a definite benefit.

An aimless or vagrant reading of God's word, or the reading of it without an object to which the reading of it is to introduce us, is as futile an effort of mind as would be the repeating of so many words in an unknown tongue. To read the Bible with the expectation that the mere act is to aid us is to treat it as we would a charm. It is the same kind of act as that of the Romanist when he kisses a crucifix or sprinkles himself with holy water. The Bible is to be consulted for the purpose of learning from it how God is to be pleased or how Christ is to be followed; its use consists in its fitness and ability to give this knowledge. If nothing is sought from it, nothing will be gained. The connection which our Lord so emphatically noticed between the acts of seeking and finding, asking and receiving, knocking and the opening of a door, applies to the study of the Bible. To find anything in it, there must be a seeking; to receive anything from it, there must be an asking; to gain access to its contents, there must be a knocking. If the professing Christian be honest in his profession, he will be able to give an answer to the question, "Why do you read your Bible?" It will be, "Because I wish to learn how I am to live as a Christian; because I earnestly desire to acquire all the instruction within my reach in regard to the type of character and the manner of life which befit me as a Christian." Such a one will crave such information as the Bible contains just as a hungry man craves food. His craving for the truth which acquaints him with God and his will will have in it all the distinctness and force of an appetite. This appetite he will bring with him to the Scriptures whenever he reads them. And Scripture truth will have a relish in it corresponding to this appetite. It may be taken as a sign of a decline in the spiritual health of any Christian when this relish for the Bible declines. The difference between a spiritual mind and a worldly mind evinces itself in one prominent way in this—that, while the latter desires not the knowledge of God, the former esteems such knowledge to be supremely valuable and is attracted to it by an instinctive affection.

If love to God be in the soul, as it must be in the case of the true believer, it will express itself as naturally as in any conceivable way, by a habit of reading the

Bible, and reading it specifically for the purpose of gaining a better acquaintance with God. The Bible will be taken up with a definite desire to learn something from it, and will be laid down with the inquiries, "What have I learned? What new views of truth have been acquired? What previous ones have been confirmed? What new emotions have been awakened, or what familiar ones have been quickened, by this reading of it?" The remark often made, "I read my Bible daily," or "I read so much of it statedly," means nothing unless it means that the reading has been conducted with direct reference to the spiritual profiting of the reader. The eyes that, seeing, see not, and the ears that, hearing, hear not, the things which God has revealed are marks of the reprobate, not of the child of God.

III.

The Bible is to be studied in a reverential spirit.

Every application of the mind to it is an exercise as truly devotional as prayer; it is literally communing with God. Those formulas, "Thus saith the Lord," "Thus spake the Spirit" or "the Holy Ghost," which are so frequent in the Scriptures, affirm that the reader is brought by these Scriptures into direct communication with the mind of God. The effect of this conviction ought to be to invest the Bible with a sacredness which cannot possibly attach to any merely human composition. Anything which serves to address the soul, however remotely, as a voice from God— as some of the stupendous objects or startling phenomena of nature—irresistibly suffuses it with a feeling of awe. The Bible is that voice speaking in articulate tones. The character which it claims for itself is that it is, as to the contents of it or the things which it reveals and teaches, a direct utterance from God. Moses and the prophets wrote it, but they wrote it by the command of God and for the purpose of giving to men the knowledge which God thought it necessary for them to possess; and the testimony which it gives, according to the Saviour's emphatic declaration (Luke xvi. 31), is entitled to a credit greater than that which would be due to one risen from the dead. What the reader of the Bible needs is always to have the sense of its sacredness present to his mind. The impressions left by its teaching will be genuine only when made with the aid and through the medium of this sense. God's voice will not have the effect of God's voice if it be not consciously recognized as his voice. It is the intelligent apprehension of this feature in the Bible that it is God's voice speaking to the reader which will make the use of it a real converse with God.

Now, this sense of the sacredness of the Bible is something which the man who seeks to find in it a rule of religious living must religiously cherish and cultivate. Familiarity with any object is known —even to a proverb—to abate the feeling of reverence with which it was at first regarded. And then the elevated frame of mind—the strain perhaps it may be called—which is implied in a feeling of reverence is apt to subside or grow lax through the effort required to maintain it. Before one is aware of it in reading the Bible the spirit may sink back from the height to which it had been lifted by the thought of God, and page after page of the divine book may be listlessly passed over without the inspiration of that thought.

This sense of the sacredness of the Bible, must, I repeat, be carefully fostered by the Christian. Just because it is one of those forms of spiritual sensibility, one of those delicate habits, which prove the perfectness of the organism in which they reside, it is easily impaired, or even lost. As the ear which is not quick to discern the distinction of sounds would never convey to the heart the peculiar force which lies in a tone of friendship or love, so the Bible, when it is not felt by the soul to be the voice of God, cannot affect the soul with the force which properly belongs to a communication from him.

IV.

The Bible is to be studied in a spirit of docility and submissiveness.

It speaks with authority. The teachings of Jesus impressed the people with the conviction that he spake in this way, and their minds, in listening to him, spontaneously assented to the truth of his doctrines and the justness of his precepts. The disposition to criticise and to controvert, in which, perhaps, we may lawfully indulge when reading an ordinary book, we should habitually repress in dealing with the Bible. Clearly, the Christian, whatever he may once have done, does not, after surrendering his faith to God, claim the right to make his own opinion the arbiter in matters of truth and righteousness. He has become the little child, and confessing his own ignorance and foolishness, and rejoicing to recognize in God a Father who cannot err and will not deceive, he looks up to him as the ultimate arbiter in all such matters. Confidence in the infallible source of his knowledge precludes all questioning and argument, because all questions are solved and all arguments are comprehended in the one conviction that the Bible is the word of God.

There is nothing unreasonable in such confidence. It is in just such confidence that the scholar takes as true what his teacher tells him is true, and the child does or refrains from doing the things which his parents command or forbid. It is only receiving as truth what comes through the testimony of One who knows, and accepting as duty what is enjoined by One who has the right to command us and who exercises his right for our interest. The all-sufficient reason, in both cases, is found in the character of him whom we trust and obey. I am assuming, of course, that the Christian, upon grounds which he deems reasonable, has accepted the Bible as a revelation from God, and that by the use of his reasonable faculties he has ascertained what is the testimony of the Bible on any given point of truth or duty. Then, I say, the act of receiving this testimony without further questioning or argument is entirely reasonable. Speculation and debate should end when God speaks. This state of mind, this docility and submissiveness of temper, of which I am speaking, is a condition essential to the profitable studying of the Scriptures. For the mind must be trustingly and lovingly placed in the hands of a teacher in order to be taught. Doubt and suspicion entertained in regard to the source from which information is sought will impair the completeness of the result, if they do not defeat it altogether. They will be like obstructions in the mouth of the vessel we are attempting to fill, or like pebbles in the mass of clay we are trying to mould into symmetrical form.

It may be added to this that the enjoyment which the mind feels in reposing with an assurance upon the trustworthiness of a teacher is necessary to a full impression of anything communicated to it. We frequently use the phrase "*resting* upon testimony," and use it in two senses—first, that of confiding in it as a genuine ground of belief; and second, that of deriving from it a sense of comfort and repose.

Where there is no "resting" in the latter of these senses, there is probably none in the former of them. Certainly, no adequate impression of the thing testified can be made upon the mind. It is the boast of the Romanist that in accepting the dogma of the infallibility of the Church he is relieved of all uneasiness or risks in his belief. To be safe he has simply to believe what the Church tells him to believe. If he can accept this dogma, he undoubtedly does experience this relief. Now, the temper in which the Romanist rests upon the testimony of the Church is that in which the Christian should rest upon the testimony of the Bible. It is *resting* which brings with it a sense of comfort and repose, and it does this because it is the resting of a true faith. In the possession of this temper the student will approach the Bible with that cordial reliance upon its truthfulness and competency, and with that freedom from all forms of strife with its teachings, which will prepare him like an empty vessel to be filled, or like the plastic clay to be moulded into figure.

The disposition I am recommending is not inconsistent with a sense of surprise in the mind of the reader at particular things with which he meets in the Bible. He may be rationally forced to admit to himself every now and then, "This is a strange incident," or "This is a hard saying;" but the obstacles of faith which a minute and shortsighted criticism might find in such enigmatical passages will disappear in a moment before the evidence for the credibility of the book which blazes like sunlight in the general facts of its history, its attributes, its contents, its aptitudes, its correspondences with the facts of life and nature, its varied uses as a factor in society, and its beneficent effects upon human character and destiny. To conclude, from the occasional features in it which we do not understand, that all this body of evidence is worthless would be as unreasonable as to affirm that a watch was no safe and useful index of time because there were parts of its structure which the observer could not see to be consistent with its plan or conducive to its result.

V.

The Bible should be read with a conviction that in it there is lodged a power to confer upon the faithful student certain and manifold benefits.

This is simply to use it as a means of grace or as one of the instrumentalities through which God is accustomed to bestow spiritual benefits. The passages which ascribe a capacity and a potency of this kind to the Scriptures are almost innumerable. David, in the nineteenth psalm, from verse 7 to verse 10, represents them as charged with an energy as diversified and as efficacious as that of the sun. They convert the soul, make wise the simple, rejoice the heart and enlighten the eyes. In Jer. xxiii. 29 the word of the Lord is likened to a fire and to a hammer that break the rock in pieces. Our Lord says (John vi. 63), "The words that I speak unto you, they are spirit, and they are life." St. Paul reminds Timothy (2 Tim. iii. 15) that the Holy Scriptures are able to make him "wise unto salvation;" and in addressing the Ephesian elders (Acts xx.

22) he commends them "to God and the word of his grace," which is able to build them up and to give them an inheritance among all them that are sanctified. Jesus, in his intercession for his disciples (John xvii. 17), prays, "Sanctify them through thy truth: thy word is truth." Such expressions must be stripped of their natural significance if we do not understand them to teach that in the Bible there is a property which is peculiar to it, and which makes it capable of communicating gracious influences to the reader using it aright, such as are not to be expected from any other book.

This property, I need hardly say, is not magical, such as an ignorant devotee supposes to belong to a consecrated candle or to the water of the Ganges. The mere use of the letter of the Bible or the mere mechanical reading of it will not secure the exercise of it. It is simply the result of God's blessing upon the honest and the earnest effort of the soul to know his will and to enjoy communion with him. The effect of a conviction of the reality of it is, not to produce superstition, but to encourage and enliven faith and to induce in the mind of the student, as often as he takes up the sacred record, the same feeling of pleasant expectancy which one carries with him when he strikes the cords of an instrument for the purpose of obtaining musical sounds, or when he opens the shutter of a dark room for the purpose of admitting light. There is implied in such a feeling a motive which looks beyond mere entertainment, or even the acquisition of knowledge, and seeks and expects from the reading of the Scriptures a spiritual refreshment and invigoration analogous to that helpful inspiration of the body which is sought and expected from the inhaling of the sea-breeze or the mountain-air. Like the blessing of the new wine which the prophet says (Isa. lxv.) 8 is found in a cluster of grapes, so it may be said to the believer, as often as he handles God's word, "Touch it thankfully, touch it hopefully; for there is a blessing in it."

VI.

With this conviction, the Christian should study the Bible with a solemn impression that he is dealing with that which the Holy Spirit uses as the means of his supernatural working.

That the soul of the Christian is the subject of this supernatural working from the beginning to the completion of its spiritual history is so clearly taught in the Scriptures that I need not pause to show the proof of the doctrine. The point with which I am concerned is the further doctrine of Scripture that it is in connection with the truths of revelation that this working is ordinarily (at least) carried on. This procedure is due to two facts—first, that the Holy Spirit operates upon the soul in accordance with, and not in violation of, the laws of its nature; and second, that it is one of these laws that the soul, in order to be in a right state, should be in agreement with the truth. To bring it into a right state, therefore—which is what the Holy Spirit undertakes to do—it must be made to see, to accept and to feel the truth.

When, for instance, the Holy Spirit would lead the soul out of a state of sinfulness into one of holiness, he must convince it that its former state is at variance with the truth, and that its latter state is in harmony with the truth; he must show it that the one is a false way and the other a right way. It is through a perception of the truth and an acknowledgment of the truth that the change is to be effected. "Thy word is truth," says the Saviour; and the word of God is the Bible. In entire consistency, therefore, with the nature of the soul, the Holy Spirit works with and through the contents of the Bible. In the use of the Bible men must seek for and expect his supernatural aid. Those right perceptions, right affections, right principles and right purposes which the Holy Spirit would implant in the heart he will introduce there by applying to the heart the truths of the Bible. And the Bible is to be read, therefore, with a constant and serious recognition of the power of the Holy Spirit as present in it and as concurrent with the exercise of reading it. Such a recognition was certainly in the Psalmist's mind when he prayed (Ps. cxix. 18), "Open thou mine eyes that I may behold wondrous things out of thy law;" and it was no less clearly in the apostle's mind when he told the Corinthians (1 Cor. ii. 14) that "the things of the Spirit of God are to be spiritually discerned," or apprehended by a discernment communicated by the Spirit; and that their faith stood not in the wisdom of man, but in the power of God, because it was in the "demonstration of the Spirit" that the gospel had been preached to them and received by them.

This connection of the Holy Spirit's influence with the use of the Bible suggests not only the habit of looking for his aid, but the duty of *asking* for it. The offices of the Holy Spirit are specially to be sought for by prayer (Luke xi. 13); hence the reading of the Bible should be accompanied with prayer for divine light. The success of the exercise, any one can see, largely depends upon the temper of mind with which the Scriptures are at any time studied and upon the manner in which the truths it presents strike the mind. Here, in determining this temper and this manner, is a place for the interposition of the Holy Spirit. A simple and earnest pleading for the benefit of this interposition will show both that the student is eagerly seeking the knowledge of God's word and that he is relying in his search, not upon the "wisdom of man" merely, but upon the "power of God." Forgetfulness of this latter duty or a presumptuous confidence in his own intellectual sufficiency may lead a man into the grave offence of "quenching the Spirit" even when professedly engaged in the study of the things of the Spirit.

VII.

The study of the Bible implies that the reading of it is followed by meditation.

It is the thinking of a thing which fastens it in the mind and causes it to take effect upon the mind. "While I was musing," says the Psalmist (Ps. xxxix. 3), "the fire burned." All that has been heretofore said of the nature and capacities of the

Bible is enough to show that there are results to be reached through the study of it which are real, and that they are worth an earnest effort to attain them. They are likened to hid treasure and deserve to be sought for by patient effort. Meditation is the precise effort of the mind, not only to uncover the contents of the Bible and to satisfy the intelligence as to whether they are there and as to what their import is, but to make them actually the possession of the student. It is the process by which we give life and force to the things which the Scripture reveals. It is not simply acquisitive, aiming to gain a knowledge of what is written, nor simply inquisitive, aiming to find out the exact value of words and meaning of propositions. It may include these or presuppose them, but it goes beyond them. It is the feeding upon food already provided and prepared rather than the providing and preparing of it. It is a sort of rumination upon what is already accepted by the mind as true and understood.

This is a complex process involving acts

of perception, memory, attention and reflective application. It requires a frank, docile, truthful and devout frame of mind. The object and the result of it are to transfer the sentiment of the Bible to the heart of the reader, so that the force of whatever kind which belongs to it shall be felt and responded to by the heart. Hence, as a rule for Christians, it may be stated that it is better to read a short portion of the Bible with due meditation than much in an unintelligent and cursory way. Some good men have adopted the plan of selecting at the beginning of each year a single verse as a motto to be kept before their minds during the year, and have found it a spring of living water affording fresh thoughts and healthful inspirations each day.

Difficulties, I am aware, in the way of connecting meditation with the reading of the Scriptures arise, sometimes from a lack of aptitude for such an exercise, of which a person is conscious, and more frequently from the sense of irksomeness which attends it. Mental work of any kind, to one not trained to it, is confessedly embarrassing and distasteful. Hence, many who read their Bibles never ponder in their hearts the things they have read. They are like the man of whom St. James speaks (i. 23) who beholds his natural face in a glass, and then goes his way and "straightway forgetteth what manner of man he was." An honest Christian, however, will feel, in the case of the word of God, that no trouble in the effort to understand it can be an excuse for declining the effort.

For the encouragement of the weak disciple it may be mentioned that the mind is very easily put under the control of regulated habit, and that the very revelation of great and inspiring truths to the soul often seems to quicken the intellect and to endow even an uncultured mind with aptitudes and energies of which it was never before conscious. Even babes, under the illumination of the Holy Spirit, may acquire the faculty of understanding things which are hid from the naturally wise and prudent.

The greatest obstacle which will beset

the duty I am recommending will probably be found, in the insatiable demands of worldly business. The Christian will be in danger of concluding that he has no time for meditating upon what he reads in the word of God, and therefore is under no obligation to concern himself with the attempt. This danger needs to be recognized and to be guarded against.

Let it be noticed that meditation is not literal reading and does not require the presence of a book, and that it is not technical study and does not require the seclusion of a closet nor the facilities of a library. It is simply the working of the mind, and may be performed, to some extent, wherever the mind is. What should prevent the performing of it, therefore, even in the place of business? Why should not some text lodged in the mind in the morning be summoned from the memory, looked at and thought over a hundred times in the day? Why should it not be at hand, like the watch in one's pocket, to be consulted from hour to hour? Even the hard seabeach over which the incoming wave rolls back again, withdrawing its volume as rapidly as it poured it in, will show here and there a cavity in which will sparkle a little pool of crystal water left by the receding tide. Surely the busiest soul, washed over merely, as it may seem to have been, by the truths of God's word which it has hurriedly surveyed, may here and there find a receptacle in which some portion of the sacred element may be retained, upon which the spirit may slake its thirst even amidst the bustle of the street or the crowding cares of the workshop or the office. At all events, the rest of the Sabbath will give to every Christian an opportunity for meditating upon the Scriptures, and the proper improvement of this opportunity will in all probability create a habit which will extend such meditation into the weekday life.

VIII.

A few suggestions as to the method of studying the Bible may be added to this exposition of the nature of the process.

FIRST. *The Bible is to be read regularly*

as a whole. The most obvious way for accomplishing this would appear to be to begin at the beginning and read it continuously through to the end. This way is very commonly pursued by religious people, and many can report that within a lifetime they have read the book through an almost incredible number of times. Such a way, however, seems to lose sight of the principle that the Bible is to be read, not for the sake of the reading of it, but for the sake of the uses which the reading of it may serve. To get a use from the reading of it, it will be found advantageous to divide it into sections and read successively a portion from each. A convenient division will be into: (1) The historical writings of the Old Testament, from Genesis to Job; (2) The poetical writings of the same, including the prophets; (3) The evangelical writings, composed of the four Gospels and the Acts; (4) The didactic writings, consisting of the Epistles and Revelation. Each reader, however, can make the division according to his own view of expediency. The object of this recommendation is to secure such a variety in the instruction obtained from the Bible as may suit the varying wants of the soul. These wants can hardly be provided for from day to day by the contents of any single one of the inspired books. Would it not be better for the reader's mind, for instance, after having been studying the structure of the tabernacle in Exodus, to turn to the confessions of the fifty-first psalm or to the touching parables of Luke xv.?

SECONDLY. *It will be an advantage to the reader to inform himself of the authorship of the book he is reading and of the circumstances of the age and country to which it relates.* Such letters as those written by St. Paul to the Corinthians can be much better understood when the mind carries along with the reading of them a clear conception of the social condition of the people to whom they were addressed. Such information can easily be obtained from the expository works which are now so numerous.

THIRDLY. *The Bible is the best interpreter of*

itself. It is an exceedingly useful practice to compare, by the aid of "marginal references," one passage with another. Such comparisons help not only to solve particular difficulties, but to bring out in an interesting way the unity of Scripture. If the truth at one point seems to be locked up in obscurity, the key to it may be found at another point, showing that the same Spirit is the author of both.

FOURTHLY. *The language of the Bible in important texts should be committed to memory.* Language is the channel through which thought and emotion flow, and a good channel facilitates the flow of thought and emotion. Scripture phrases coming readily to the mind are thus aids to devotion. They furnish the wheels upon which the soul moves most comfortably and safely in prayer.

FIFTHLY. *It is **well frequently** to arrest the mind at certain points and compel it to reflect that it is dealing not merely with a book, but with facts; not merely with poetic conceits or abstract propositions, but with living truths.* Let the thought often challenge the attention of the reader: "The Jehovah who spake to Moses is the God who still speaks to me;" "The Jesus who conversed with Nicodemus is still uttering the same doctrine to me." Such a habit will serve to bring home the teachings of the Bible to the reader personally.

SIXTHLY. *It is an adventitious, but not an improper, aid in studying the Bible to invest particular parts and passages of it with associations which are precious to the reader.* By this process human history becomes interwoven with the word of God, and the sacred volume becomes dearer to us because enshrined in sacred recollections and experiences: "This book or this chapter brings back the image of a sainted parent whose tongue was wont to recite it with rapturous tones in my youthful ears;" "This verse contains the sunbeam which led a distinguished reformer or evangelist out of darkness into light;" "This fragment of a psalm became a song of triumph on a martyr's lips;" "This gracious promise brought the balm of consolation to my heart long years ago when crushed with the weight of some great sorrow;" "This petition is perfumed with the memory of some pious friend whose panting after God it expressed;" "This vision of the heavenly city revealed its opened gates and shining streets to the eye of some sufferer amidst the agonies of a dying-bed." It is wonderful how many things in the life of an individual may thus link themselves to the holy book, and may throw around it the drapery of sweet and tender thoughts and feelings. Thus it may be made what no other book can be—a personal friend, a sharer in our private joys and sorrows, a kinsman dividing with us the secret life of the soul. Such associations, like a chime of holy earth-born melodies blending with the voice of God, deserve to be cherished, as they both add to the attractiveness and enhance the efficiency of the Bible.

CHAPTER IV.

OBSERVANCE OF PUBLIC WORSHIP.

CHRIST was so conspicuously a worshiper of God and an attendant upon public worship that no one can be a follower of him without imitating him in this respect. Besides his example, he has given his disciples a form of prayer, and a form which seems to imply that they will worship in companies. Indeed, it may be asked how any one can believe that the Lord is "great and greatly to be praised," as every believer in Christ must, without being moved in some outspoken way to magnify and praise him.

The mere act and the mere word of worship are, we know, of no value in his sight. Without the spirit and the understanding, our oblations are vain and our incense is an abomination unto him (Isa. i.

13). But the fact that the offering of formal worship without the participation of the soul is an offence to God does not prove that formal worship in which the soul does participate is not acceptable to God and may be required by him.

The proper definition of the word "worship" is "the acknowledgment by one party of the *worth* of another." The worship of the Almighty is the acknowledgment by man of God's infinite worth. Worth is entitled to recognition wherever it is found. Not to recognize it is evidence, in any party, of moral blindness or obliquity, and is an exhibition of injustice which is positively criminal. The duty of worshiping God is only the active phase of the duty of believing in God.

Hear how the Scriptures speak of him: "O Lord our Lord, how excellent is thy name in all the earth" (Ps. viii. 11); "Worthy is the Lamb that was slain, to receive power and riches and wisdom and strength and honor and glory and blessing," is said of our Lord Jesus Christ (Rev. v. 12).

Excellence and worth so transcendant

are entitled to receive proper acknowledgment at the hands of men. How can a man be a religious man without acknowledging them? The only question that can possibly be entertained is, "How are such excellence and such worth to be acknowledged?"

The answer to this question is, first, by an intelligent apprehension of them and a complacent appreciation of them by the soul. The organ of acknowledgment must undoubtedly be an enlightened and approving soul. But the utterance in some formal way of what the soul believes and feels is always a natural exercise, and is—ordinarily, at least—a condition necessary to distinctness of belief and vividness of feeling. Hence, to this first answer a second is to be joined: God's excellence and worth are to be acknowledged in every formal way in which the soul can express its belief in and its feeling toward them. The act, the word, the sensible demonstration, constituted as man now is, are co-ordinate factors with the thought and the emotion, and help, with the latter, to call out and to call forth the life of the soul. Man is not yet capable of living as a pure spirit, and needs the aid of formal expression to keep up his sense of God's excellence and worth. So long as the expression serves this purpose— really serves it, and serves no other purpose—it is a valuable help, not to say a necessary one, to spiritual life. Public worship is such an expression, or, rather, a combination of such expressions. Properly conducted, it is a celebration of God's excellence and worth. It is enjoined, not because God needs the praise of man, but because it is due from man, becoming in man and profitable to man.

So far as appears from Scripture, God has always been worshiped by formal rites. These rites are the monuments by which he asserts his claim to faith and reverence and honor in the eyes of an apostate world. They are the testimony in behalf of religion which he causes to be proclaimed in the ears of the unbelieving generations of men. For a Christian to disown his obligation to attend upon the public worship of God is to discredit these monuments and to contradict this testimony. To say that he does not need the influence of it himself is to betray an ignorance of the wants of his own soul; to say that the world does not need it is to exhibit an indifference to the wants of his race. Such incongruities will be shunned by every honest follower of Christ. As the Son of God, during his human life, kept the holy days and frequented the synagogue and the temple as a faithful Israelite, no man claiming to be his disciple can conscientiously fail to keep the Christian Sabbath and frequent the place where God is worshiped according to the law of the New Testament.

I.

The observance of public worship ought to be classed by the young Christian among those moral duties which he has engaged to perform. It rests upon an ordinance of God as distinctly as do the commands which require him to be honest and charitable in his dealings with his neighbor. It is a part of the peculiar work which is given him as a professor of religion to do. It is not something left to the taste or the fancy or the convenience of the individual; it is what the Lord expects from every one of his servants. He evidently requires his worship to be maintained in the world: "Ye shall keep my Sabbaths, and reverence my sanctuary: I am the Lord" (Lev. xxvi. 2).

Now, by whom is this to be done? "By the church," it may be answered; yet what is the church but the aggregate of the living men and women in any generation or community? Let these living men and women neglect the worship of God, and where is the church which will keep it up? The church is realized in each one of these men and women, and the obligations of the church rest upon each one of them. The divine ordinance which calls for a worshiping church is simply a call to each church-member to be a worshiper. Let the church-member remember this, and from the moment of his entering the church let him place this duty foremost among those forms of business to which his life is to be devoted.

I use the term "business" in this connection because I have observed that what is technically called "business" is the most frequent obstacle in the way of the performance of this duty of public worship. The excuse which in his own view most effectually justifies a man in neglecting this duty is that his "business" forbids it. He would be ashamed to say that his pleasure or his indolence forbade it, but "business" has something respectable—almost sacred—in it; for is not he who provides not for his own said to be worse than an infidel? (1 Tim. v. 8.)

The mistake here is in making a distinction between business and the worship of God. The Christian's business comprehends the doing of all his heavenly Father's will, and it is as much his heavenly Father's will that his worship should be observed by his people as that their families should be supported by diligence in their secular callings. If any distinction is to be made between the two, the former should take precedence of the latter; the business which concerns God should claim attention before that which concerns man. The Saviour directed an unsparing rebuke at this disposition to place devotion to worldly business over religious duty when he said to the rich young man (Matt. xix. 21), "Go sell that thou hast, and come and follow me." Worldly business must retire when religious business presents its claims. The man too busy at his counter or in his office or his workshop to attend upon the worship of God is in the most notorious sense a neglecter of his business as a Christian.

The same is true of the man who excuses himself from attendance upon Sabbath worship on the ground that on the Sabbath his overtaxed mind and his weary body are unfit to participate in its services. Has he a right so to disqualify himself for God's business, by overtaxing his mind and by wearying his body in the prosecution of his own calling? There is a use of "the mammon of unrighteousness," the Saviour teaches (Luke xvi. 9), which can make "friends" to the believer or helpers in securing admittance for him to "everlasting habitations," but surely it cannot be such a use as robs God of the service due to him. Oh, let the follower of Christ be warned of this device of Satan, and let him see to it that in his devotion to his worldly business he does not become a defaulter to his Master. His success in his religious life will largely depend upon his fidelity in this particular.

The ordinary occupations of life create a perpetual drain upon spiritual strength. Worship—public worship—is needed to repair the waste. Not only the Sabbath services, but the lecture and the prayer-meeting of the week, are needed for this purpose. These religious episodes are tonics to the soul. They meet the Christian in the midst of his working-days with solaces as timely and as refreshing as those which the Israelites found in the wells and the palm trees of Elim: "They that wait upon the Lord shall renew their strength" (Isa. xl. 21). The habit of attending upon public worship, once formed, will cause the difficulties which obstruct it to vanish, and will make an abundant compensation for all the effort it costs, both in the relief it will give to the sense of duty and in the supply it will furnish to the needs of the soul.

II.

The worshiping of God is so serious a business that it calls for forethought and preparation.

The disposition to engage in it as a mere matter of routine or custom, without a conscious impression of its meaning, may easily arise from the fact that the mind is so often called to the performance of the duty. Week after week, Sabbath after Sabbath, throughout the year, at a regular hour, the worshiper is summoned to the house of God. That each occasion should present itself with a fresh interest and should stir the heart with a felt attractiveness, it is necessary that the attention should be directed to the work in hand and that the soul should be strung, by a process of reflection, with well-tuned chords. Levity of mind is, of course, at open variance with the idea of worship; vacancy of mind is hardly less so. With good reason, therefore, the counsel was given by them of old time: "Be not rash with thy mouth, and let not thine heart be hasty to utter anything before God" (Eccl. v. 21). What is said and what is done in worship ought to be said and done with deliberation, in a religious spirit and with a religious intent. As no man rationally enters upon a grave enterprise without contemplating the nature of it and the mental conditions it requires in the party engaging in it, so the Christian should seriously strive to put himself in frame for such an act as the worship of God. He should never precipitate himself into it in a rash or hasty manner.

Very obviously, in this endeavor after self-preparation, he should by prayer invoke those gracious inspirations which come from Him with whom are "the preparation of the heart, and the answer of the tongue" (Prov. xvi. 1). No truly devout man will fail to take account of his own infirmities when he proposes to approach God in worship. The promised aids of the Holy Spirit will never seem more seasonable than then, and they will be definitely sought by prayer.

In this connection it may not be amiss to say that in churches where liturgies are not used in public worship there is a special call for effort and culture on the part of the individual engaging in the work. While it is the task of the minister to direct the current of devotion, it is the task of the hearer, in order to be a worshiper, to throw his mind into that current. This requires closeness of attention and control of thought. The invitation, "Let us pray," should be responded to by each worshiper with the determination to make the prayer about to be uttered his own. In the reading of the Scriptures it is undoubtedly an aid to the object in view for the hearer to have his own Bible at hand and to follow the officiating minister.

The service of psalmody is emphatically the service of the people. It is the duty of every church-member as far as possible to take part in it. The objection of inability, so often raised, only lays the ground for another remark—viz., that it is the duty of every church-member to make it a study to be able to take part in it. It belongs to his business as a Christian man to educate himself for this work, and, if he be a parent, to educate his children for it. It is a perversion of this divine ordinance when the congregation delegates the execution of it to a choir, and, instead of singing praise to God, expect to be sung to themselves. Rightly considered, there is as much reason for the petition, "Lord, teach us to sing," as there is for the petition, "Lord, teach us to pray;" for singing is essentially the same act as praying. There is room for the question whether the absence of spiritual power which is so frequently deplored in our churches is not due to the failure of Christian people to do their duty in this branch of worship. Certainly, a company of professed worshipers indolently sitting in their pews to be entertained by a musical performance are more likely to repel than to invite the offices of the divine Inspirer.

III.

The spirit of worship should be as distinctly carried into the hearing of the word preached as into the purely devotional parts of the service.

It is a mistake, and a hurtful one, to suppose that in listening to the sermon we have ceased to maintain communion with God. It is he who has then become the party speaking, and it may be that in the utterances then and there addressed to us he may make a response to the very aspirations which have ascended to him in our praises and prayers.

The distinction which is sometimes made between the formally devotional service and the sermon in public worship, and the tone of depreciation with which the latter is, in certain quarters, spoken of, are the offspring of ignorance. The teaching of the law of the Lord seems always to have been closely associated with the worship of God, and the reason for the connection is founded in the nature of religion. Worship, to be a religious act, must be the expression of right views, convictions and feelings in regard to God; without these it is an empty and a worthless ceremony. These it is the office of preaching to supply and to cultivate. Instruction in the things of God is the natural purveyor of the material required for devotion, and in its work goes hand in hand with literal worship. And, conversely, it may be said that preaching needs the aid of worship. Without it the instructions of the pulpit may enrich the intelligence without exciting the spiritual affections; with it they plant themselves in the soul as quickened forms of faith, and become real and vital forces through the medium of speech and emotion. The work of the minister, therefore, wisely comprehends both functions—that of directing the devotions of the people, and that of preaching to them the word of God.

The hearing of the word preached is to be attended to with substantially the same frame of mind as that with which direct worship is to be performed. The object of the preacher, if he understands his calling, is to report and to give effect to the truth which God has revealed; the duty of the hearer is to get, through the preacher, a better knowledge and a clearer impression of this truth. The thing which the preacher has to do is to deliver a message from God; the business of the hearer is to look for it, appropriate it and carry it away with him. In order to this, the counsels given in a previous chapter in regard to the study of the Bible may profitably be followed.

In addition, I would offer the following suggestions:

First. The worshiper should examine himself before going to the house of God as to his motive and purpose, and should endeavor to make it his definite errand to honor God and to obtain religious instruction. This process is an easy one, within the power of everybody, and is necessary in order to make "going to church" a rational act.

Second. The ear and the heart should be prepared by prayer for the parts they are to take in the service.

Third. Peculiarities in the preacher, favorable or unfavorable, should not be suffered to divert the mind from the appreciation of the truth presented. A genuine appetite will relish food even when conveyed in a homely vessel, and will never miss the food through admiration of an attractive vessel.

Fourth. After the hearing of the sermon the mind should be questioned as to the profit gained by a review of its contents and by meditation upon them.

Fifth. The impression of the word preached should be fixed and deepened by conversation upon it with other serious persons.

Sixth. Prayer for the quickening influences of the Holy Spirit should be offered up, that the seed sown may take root in the hearer's heart and bring forth appropriate fruit.

By efforts like these the preaching of the word may be expected to become what it was designed to be—a means of edification, a source of sanctifying grace and an invaluable help to the Christian seeking to understand the will and to acquire the mind of his Master. The faithful hearing of God's word is enough like prayer to be entitled to a share in all the promises made to prayer, and the man who goes to it, as he goes to his knees, asking from God the bread of life, may be sure he will never be sent away empty.

"What man is there of you, whom if his son ask bread, will he give him a stone?" (Matt. vii. 9.)

CHAPTER V.

PRIVATE PRAYER.

THE professor of religion who does not pray in private is no more the being which that title describes than is the infant, who has never breathed, a living child. It is impossible to know God, to believe in him and to love him, without holding intercourse with him by definite and intelligent acts of the soul.

The arguments by which the reasonableness and the utility of prayer to God are demonstrated are numerous and sufficient to satisfy any ingenuous mind. But the necessity for argument is superseded here by the fact that man is constrained to pray by the moral constitution which naturally belongs to him. Language of entreaty or deprecation oftentimes instinctively bursts from the lips of those who have denied the being of a God and have been wont to laugh at the folly of those who prayed to him.

Indeed, so potent is the law by which men are impelled to pray that under its conscious pressure they are liable to be carried into excesses in their practice of the duty. Their need of prayer is felt at so many points that it seeks to relieve itself by multiplying objects to which prayer can be addressed. Hence, the heathen have invented as many divinities as there are departments of nature and life with which their well-being is connected. Not satisfied with the idea of one god—the all-sufficient object upon which a rational faith is content to rest—they have amplified that idea until it includes as many gods as a superstitious fancy is pleased to invent.

In the same way, the Romish Church, with that consummate sagacity which it has displayed in using every avenue by which the hearts of men may be reached and controlled, has taken advantage of this natural disposition to pray, and has fed and stimulated it by encouraging its members to address their devotions to the saints, to the angels and to the Virgin Mary. The readiness with which these false modes of prayer gain circulation proves that there is a genuine thing of which these are counterfeits, and that in man's nature there is a foundation laid for the use of that thing.

The religious man will be prompted to pray, *first*, because of a propensity belonging to him as a man; and *second*, because this propensity has had a new incitement and a new direction given to it by the new spiritual life which has been imparted to him. The very impulses of his mind and heart in reference to God will take on the form of prayer; so that there is literal truth in the familiar line,

> "Prayer is the Christian's vital breath."

And as every affection residing in the soul is strengthened by expression and nourishes itself, as it were, by the terms it uses in giving itself utterance, so the religious affections need the channel of articulate prayer to keep themselves vigorous and fresh in the believer's soul. A decline in spiritual life will follow a neglect of prayer just as certainly as a plant decays when the necessary moisture is withdrawn from its roots.

Still further, the connection which the Scriptures establish between prayer and the positive blessing of God makes the practice of it a necessity for the Christian coextensive with his wants. Religious living is a life of entire dependence upon God. That he is an independent agent is one of the illusions under which the natural man lives. He is flattered and deceived by the thought that he is equal to his needs and capable of being the conservator and the architect of his own happiness. It is the characteristic of the spiritual man to find—and to delight to find—all his sufficiency in God. There is such a connection between his daily bread, for instance, and the providence of God that in his toiling for it he sees the propriety of asking God to give it; and when he has gained it by his toiling, he still feels bound to give God thanks for it.

Men's needs at all times run in advance of their own resources or carry them beyond their depth, and so prompt them to call for help outside of and above themselves. The godless man resists this prompting; the religious man gladly assents to it, and sees among the conditions of success in all his undertakings such a concurrent working of God as presents a definite thing to be prayed for. The convictions which characterize him as a Christian will make him a man of prayer. Christ was pre-eminently this, and those who follow him must be like him in this respect. It is so necessary that the young church-member should pray, and that his praying should be an exercise of the heart, that I would enjoin upon him the following counsels.

I.

Let it be YOURSELF *who prays.*

By this I mean let prayer be the genuine expression of what you feel and desire; let your soul be in it. Words, when the soul is in them, are the outgoings of the man himself; where it is not in them, they are but sound—a mechanical result which a flute could produce. You and the want you bring to God must be one. It was so with the prodigal son; the shame and the wretchedness under which he was perishing exactly reported themselves in the words he addressed to his father. It was so with the Syrophœnician woman; her daughter's suffering was a source of an agony to her own heart, and all the apparent repulses of the Saviour could not check the cry, "Lord, help me."

In any extreme position of danger or distress it is easy to see that the whole man is in the desire for relief and will be equally in the prayer that asks for it. It is this presence of self in your prayers which makes them prayers. If they are not yours, they are not prayers at all. The repeating of the best form in the world, where it is not inspired by your own soul, is not praying. Merely to "*say* your prayers" is to utter "sayings," not prayers.

On this account it is well, before engaging in the act of prayer, to pause for a moment to interrogate the mind as to the objects it is about to present to God, and as to the sincerity of the desires it professes to entertain for them.

It is well, further, to learn to express your prayers in words of your own.

This need not be a difficult task. Ordinarily, you do not depend upon others to give you the phrases in which you express your thoughts and your feelings. Indeed, such is the law of the mind that in the very process of defining a thought or a feeling to itself it has already clothed it in words. When the Saviour, wearied with his journey, sat by the well at Sychar, he said to the woman who came to draw water, "Give me to drink." Any one suffering in the same way could, and would, have said the same. A definite wish is easily put into language; study is not needed and art would be out of place in the articulating of it. "I thirst" is the feeling of which consciousness takes notice in a case like that of our Lord's; "Give me to drink" is the form of that feeling expressing itself to another in prayer. The

"I" of the feeling reappears in the "me" of the prayer.

The subject of a feeling can best express that feeling. The simplicity with which it is expressed is no fault. The style of a prayer is a matter of secondary importance. For the construction of a prayer the soul wants no rule but the rule of truthfulness; and the more plain and direct the form of it may be, the more it may correspond with this rule. No one man can so completely represent another, and so anticipate all his experiences, as to be able beforehand to prepare a set of prayers which shall cover all the circumstances and meet all the needs of the latter. In using the prayer of another there would seem to be more likelihood that the self which must be the speaker should be absent than when the speaker is using his own words.

Forms, however, are not to be absolutely condemned; they may often be employed with advantage. Especially, the Scripture phrases, which are so wonderfully adapted to the conditions of the human soul, give us an invaluable aid in moulding into prayer the desires of the heart. Only let it be always borne in mind that another man's prayer can become yours simply by throwing yourself into it. The dialect of prayer is the dialect of nature. Above all things seek to be natural—that is, simple and truthful—in your prayers; and to this end first define your desires to your own mind, and then tell them to God in just the form in which you have defined them to your own mind.

II.

In your praying PRAY TO GOD.

When a man speaks, he must have a person before him; for speech is the communication of thought, and communication requires a receiver as well as a giver. Prayer to God implies that he is the Hearer of what is spoken—not merely in the sense in which he must hear everything as an omniscient being, but in the sense of a being made consciously present and intentionally addressed by the mind of the speaker. It is quite possible that prayer, so called, should not be made to God at all—that is, it is quite possible that men should professedly pray where God's presence is not discerned by their minds, and where the words spoken are not directed to him personally. They may bend the knee and then occupy themselves with self-communings, with a sort of pious soliloquy or reverie, and fancy they are praying. They are really here thinking aloud, as it were—a process in which the mind is reacting upon itself instead of transacting with God. So, in their addresses to God, and while using his adorable names and titles, they may only be addressing an abstract and imaginary object.

It is a natural habit of the mind to personify its own conceptions. Orators and poets avail themselves of it in order to give vividness to what they are remembering or what they are trying to realize. When Cowper wrote those tender lines,

> "My mother! when I learned that thou wast dead,
> Say, wast thou conscious of the tears I shed?
> Hovered thy spirit o'er thy sorrowing son?
> Wretched e'en then, life's journey just begun?"

he was simply indulging in affectionate

reminiscences, speaking of a thing of the past, not speaking to a thing of the present. When Milton, in his "Paradise Lost," utters the invocation, "Sing, heavenly Muse!" he was not speaking to a person, but attempting to rouse the energies of his own soul by personifying them.

A similar illusion may be practised upon ourselves in praying to God. Certain thoughts about God may be thrown into the form of an address to God, but thoughts about God are not prayer to God. Prayer must put us literally in the position of one person speaking to another person.

Of course this cannot be, in our case, a face-to-face communion with God, as it is said to have been in the case of Moses, but it is a spirit-to-spirit communion. And, as there is no appeal to the senses here, it is the mind itself which must make God a visible person; through the medium of faith it must see "Him who is invisible." Hence the mind must be put in a position to see him by deliberate forethought and by a constant fixing of the eye of the soul upon God during prayer.

Every praying person is familiar with the tendency of the mind to wander in prayer, and every sincere worshiper deplores this and feels it to be sin. The explanation of this experience is that for the time the person has ceased to see God and to speak to God, and so has ceased to pray.

Let the Christian who is in earnest guard against putting this similitude of prayer in the place of the real thing. There is no prayer which is not the converse of the soul with God—no prayer where the thought, the feeling, the desire, does not consciously reach God; and, seeing how hard it is to lift the weak earthly spirit of man to this high communion, there is ample reason for a resort to that aid of the Holy Spirit of which the apostle speaks (Rom. viii. 26): "The Spirit also helpeth our infirmities; for we know not what we should pray for as we ought, but the Spirit itself maketh intercession for us with groanings which cannot be uttered."

III.

In praying, be careful, while you pray, TO DO NO MORE THAN PRAY.

To pray is to beg, to take the attitude of one soliciting a favor; it is something, therefore, quite different from demanding or prescribing or enjoining. It properly excludes the assertion of a right on the part of the petitioner, for what is a man's by right is his by debt. It is what the party applied to is bound to pay. It is not with the tone of demand that man is to address God; prayer is an expression of man's need, not of God's duty. The ground upon which it is to be offered is God's willingness to regard man's need, not an obligation requiring him to relieve it.

Now, it is not to be supposed that any man would deliberately command the services of God, and yet he may proximately do this in various ways; as when he forgets that God may properly say "No" to his petition; or when he presumes to dictate the time and the manner in which his prayer is to be answered; or when he insists upon being gratified in his desires at the expense of God's will; or when he has no intention to use for God's glory the favor asked; or when he prays in such a temper as shall make him feel wronged in the event of God's appearing to withhold the blessing sought.

It is evident that the spirit in which prayer is to be made is one of profound humility. It is that of a beggar casting his needs at the footstool of a benevolent, but at the same time a wise and righteous, sovereign. The truly Christian man will always pray under the subduing and restraining influence of this spirit: he will be the suppliant, not the exactor; and, with whatever earnestness and importunity he may urge his requests, he will remember that in regard to the disposal of the matters to which they relate there are many things which he must leave to the good-pleasure of God. The Saviour's prayer in Gethsemane should teach his followers to couple the significant formula "If it be possible" with their most ardent appeals to God.

IV.

Let your prayers be accompanied WITH CORRESPONDING ACTS. *In other words, act in accordance with your prayers.*

You will do this, for instance, when you patiently watch and wait for the results of your prayers. You do not pray in the spirit of the man who presents a check for which he expects instantaneously to receive the amount of money called for, nor in that of the man who drops his bucket into a well looking for it immediately to return filled with water. You have simply stated your wants and your troubles to God, and have referred the solution of them to him. To his judgment you have left the questions as to whether it is expedient that your request should be granted at all, and whether, if granted, the answer should come at the time or in the form which you have proposed. You have avowed your confidence in him by thus appealing to God; you will avow it still further by subsequently maintaining an attitude of expectancy before him.

This latter act of confidence seems necessary to prove the reality of the former. Who, seeking admittance to a house, would knock at the door and then go away forgetting what he had done? By waiting for something to result from it he who truly knocks in prayer will show that he meant something by knocking. This outlooking frame of mind, if cultivated, would undoubtedly have the double effect of deepening the believer's sense of his dependence on God and of revealing to him innumerable instances in which his dependence is met and relieved by the orderings of God's providence.

Another of those acts which should concur with prayer is the diligent using of all practicable means for securing the blessing sought. No reasonable man expects miracles to be wrought in his behalf, and no reasonable man would claim to be credited as sincere in asking God for a particular benefit, when he was unwilling to make an effort on his own part to gain it. A man's working must go along with his praying. God "giveth seed to the sower," not to the sluggard: "The husbandman that laboreth must be first partaker of the fruits" (2 Tim. ii. 6). A Christian's life ought to be the repetition of his prayers, and no really religious man will expect a blessing from God, either temporal or spiritual, unless by corresponding acts he is laboring to secure the blessing. The result of such an accordance would probably be that his life would be better and his prayers more frequently successful.

It may be added, as a further thought in this connection, that the man who prays in a right spirit will not limit his praying to the mere asking of favors from God. The same spirit that asks a favor under the stress of a want or a danger will lead a man to express gratitude for favors already received, to feel and confess his sins which make him unworthy of what he asks, and to render adoring ascriptions of praise to those glorious attributes and offices of God by which he offers himself to his people as their Refuge in all their times of trouble.

V.

Let your prayers be offered always with a distinct REFERENCE TO CHRIST *as your medium of access to God, as the ground of your hope of acceptance with him, and as the High Priest through whose hands your petitions are presented to the Father.*

While it is true that men are naturally constrained to pray to God, it is equally true that they are naturally repelled in their approach to him by a sense of their ill-desert. The prophet's question (Mic. vi. 6), "Wherewith shall I come before the Lord, and bow myself before the high God?" is one which every member of a sinful race will feel obliged to ask. This "Wherewith" is supplied in the mediation of Christ. Every earnest worshiper will thankfully recognize the fitness of this provision of the gospel to his wants. The name of Christ has been left by him to his followers as a passport to the throne of grace. It furnishes them with both a warrant and an encouragement to pray. It associates them with Christ in their praying, enables them to join hands, as it were, with him as their Elder Brother in drawing near to God, and so inspires them with that sense of sonship or filial trustfulness which Paul declares to be the privilege of every believer: "Ye have not received the spirit of bondage again to fear, but ye have received the spirit of adoption, whereby we cry, Abba, Father" (Rom. viii. 15).

VI.

Let the practical question, HOW IS THIS PRACTICE OF PRAYER TO BE KEPT UP? *be early considered and answered.*

As men are ordinarily situated, this question will seem to present a discouraging enigma. To many persons—perhaps to the majority—the performance of the duty it proposes will appear an utter impossibility. How can the man or the woman pursued each day, from morning to night, by the exactions of business or by the cares of the household find either time or capacity for such intercourse with God as I have been describing? The difficulty is a real one, and it is well for the professor of religion to look at it and to dispose of it at an early period. There is an advantage in promptly dealing with it. With the view of reducing it somewhat, the following suggestions are offered.

First. Beware of admitting the idea that the difficulties which lie in the way of practicing private prayer are an excuse for abandoning it. It is by "enduring hardness"—that is, by encountering and overcoming difficulties—that you are to show yourself "a good soldier of Jesus Christ." Difficulties lie all along the path of the Christian's life, and it is by his endeavors to surmount them that he will give the best evidence of the genuineness of his faith and of the earnestness of his purpose.

Second. Put the necessity for prayer in the same class with the necessity for your daily food. A margin of time will always be found for the reception of the latter; cannot a similar margin be found for the practice of the former? A brief season only is required for prayer when the heart is in it. Let this be borrowed from the morning before the day's work begins, or from the night before you retire to sleep.

Third. During the day, if no opportunity for deliberate prayer can be found, try to form the habit of mentally holding communion with God. It is possible to keep God so constantly in the view of the soul that he may be consulted at any time by a glance, just as the mariner makes his way across the ocean by perpetually watching the compass. Especially in any critical juncture it is a wise custom and a helpful resource to make these quick appeals to God, and so to go into every conflict with temptation consciously clad in a divine panoply. Thus Nehemiah (Neh. ii. 4), when serving King Ahasuerus as cupbearer, before he ventured to proffer his request to be permitted to visit Jerusalem, secretly "prayed to the God of heaven."

It is an unspeakable comfort to the truly godly man that God can be addressed so easily, without formal adjuncts, but it needs to be added that the habit of so addressing him can hardly be kept alive without sometimes resorting to the aid of the closet and the spoken word. It is not the bended knee nor the devout phrase which makes the prayer, but still, as natural expressions of what the soul is doing in prayer, these are such helps to the spirit of prayer that without them the latter is apt to languish or to expire altogether.

CHAPTER VI.

THE CULTIVATION OF PERSONAL RELIGION.

THERE is a work to be done by the Christian which is distinct from that which belongs to him in his capacity as a member of the church. It is that of *cultivating religion in his own soul*.

The obligation to do this work naturally lies upon all men. In joining the church a man acknowledges this obligation, and at the same time acknowledges his sin in having previously neglected it and avows his purpose in the future faithfully to discharge it. It was in part to aid men in doing this work that the Church was instituted, and church-membership, and even zeal in complying with church rules and rites, will avail nothing where this is overlooked. Religious living cannot exist where there is not religion in the heart. The living of any man, no matter how it may be made to look, will really be what the man himself is. The stream which attracts the observer's eye must spring from a fountain concealed within the hidden rock, and in its character will partake of the quality of that fountain. A religious life will be an impossibility unless the springs of life within the soul are tinctured and stirred by religious principles and motives.

The follower of Christ must never forget that in order practically to follow him he must be subjectively or internally like him: "If any man have not the spirit of Christ, he is none of his" (Rom. viii. 9). The Spirit of Christ is an indwelling power determining the attributes and the disposition of the man himself. Its presence will be attested by a process of growth or transformation by which the man will be more and more shaped into the form and developed into the stature of a perfect man in Christ Jesus. It would be a fatal mistake to imagine that one is born into the kingdom of God full-grown, or that admission to a church seals his salvation and absolves him from all further concern about his spiritual condition. The assuming of membership in the church is not the completion, but the beginning, of a work. Or, rather, it is the continuing of a work which had been begun before in the assuming of a new relation to God by the believer through his faith in the Lord Jesus Christ. That prior relation must be maintained by care, exercise and culture after he has entered the church. All the outward badges which may be put upon him will not make him what he ought to be as a member of the church—that is, a child of God. It was as a man already religious that he took on him the vows involved in a public profession of religion. As a religious man he is possessed of a new nature, evincing itself by peculiar affections toward God; and the vows involved in his public profession require him to keep this new nature in a healthy and an active condition. He is to cultivate it by attentions as direct as those he bestows upon a plant he wishes to rear, or as those by which he seeks to educate his child into a becoming manhood.

The true children of God or members of

his Church have their type in "the tree planted by the rivers of water, bringing forth its fruit in its season" (Ps. i. 3)—that is, in a living and growing organism, and not in the dead columns standing in stately symmetry along the aisles of a cathedral. It is life—the "life of God in the soul"—which makes the Christian; and the first duty of the follower of Christ is to attend to the cultivation of this life, or, what is the same thing, to "working out his own salvation with fear and trembling."

I.

In doing this it is evidently necessary that he should give a prominent place to the idea that *he is standing always in direct contact with God*, so that all his religious movements may be said consciously to terminate upon him as their object.

God should be, in a supreme sense, the One with whom he has to do, the One with whom his soul is perpetually transacting. His standard of character, his rules of duty, the motives of his conduct, the quarter to which his responsibilities point, and from which conscience derives its judgments and its verdicts, should distinctively be found in God. It is only by maintaining this intimate and constant association with God that any man can be religious. It is just as impossible to imbue the soul with the spirit of piety without keeping it exposed to the shining of God's face as it is impossible to give color to a flower without the aid of the sun's ray. It is not enough to make a fellow-man—not even the best Christian you know—your model. It is not enough to make the terms of a decent standing in a church the measure of your religiousness. Whatever diverts the mind from God as the Being whom we are striving specially to please, and upon whose approbation we depend as the ultimate source of our satisfaction, is adapted to stifle rather than to foster the religious spirit. The right-minded child is the one who always keeps foremost in his view the tribunal of his home, over which the parent presides, and who feels that he is true to his obligations only so long as he puts that above the opinions of his companions and the canons of society.

In the same way, God's children must recognize the paramount authority of their home-tribunal, and must seek their peace in the commendation which their heavenly Father breathes upon them in the solitude of his presence-chamber. Such habitual dwelling with God will be religious living, and a living in an atmosphere where the principle of the religious life will be sure to grow.

II.

That reasonable solicitude which any one would feel in regard to an undertaking of a worldly sort in which he was interested ought to be exercised by the Christian in regard to the spiritual prosperity of his soul.

His bodily health, we know, is an object of concern to every man. It requires thought, circumspection, prudence, oversight; and with persons who act reasonably it receives all these. It is anxiously watched over from day to day, and any deviation from a sound condition is noted and the remedy for it sought and applied. The sincere Christian will inspect his religious condition just as carefully and closely. He has a character and a standing to maintain in reference to God, just as he has in reference to the community among whom he lives; and as he guards these with jealous vigilance in respect to the latter relation, so he will in respect to the former. He will "*study* to show himself approved unto God" just as he *studies* to preserve a good reputation in the sight of his neighbors. He will never suffer himself to fall into indifference or recklessness in regard to his religious state, nor indolently take it for granted that all is right within him. While he sleeps thus the enemy may be sowing tares amongst the wheat which he has pledged himself to produce.

St. Paul's proposal to Barnabas (Acts xv. 36), "Let us go again and visit our brethren in every city where we have preached the word of the Lord, and *see how they do*"—or *fare*, as the word means—indicates a work which every Christian needs to perform for himself. He is to go again and again and see how his soul is faring. Other interests must not be allowed to interrupt his watchfulness over this superlative one.

The sad lament of the Bride in the Song of Solomon (i. 6), "They made me keeper of the vineyards, but mine own vineyard have I not kept," might be made by many a follower of Christ who has been led to neglect his spiritual estate in his absorbing devotion to his secular concerns. The world is a hard master and will urge its claims with an unsparing rigor. Its exactions must be resisted, or the Christian's own "vineyard" will suffer damage. It is true there is a possibility of an excessive attention to the frames and workings of the soul. Some men practice this introspection or self-anatomy to such a degree that they fall into a morbid state of mind and lose the power of accurate discernment. The results in such cases are hurtful because of the abuse of a mode of treatment which when properly applied is right and wholesome. But that some caring for, some watching over, some keeping of, his own vineyard or his own religious state, by the Christian is a necessary condition of his spiritual health and prosperity is undeniable.

III.

The positive methods by which piety may be expected to be fostered in the heart ought to be diligently made use of by the professor of religion.

Every faculty, every aptitude, of man is capable of culture and attains perfection through culture. "In grace" men may "grow," as in other things; and growth means progress, development, advancement from stage to stage—a process which, in the nature of it, may be helped or retarded by favoring or opposing circumstances. The Christian will grow in grace by faithfully using all legitimate means of grace. For instance,

1. He will seek to enlarge his religious knowledge, for in any department knowledge is an aid to efficiency. To this end he will avail himself of the instruction offered through the Scriptures, the pulpit and the lecture-room, and the various forms of religious literature.

2. He will seek to keep his religious affections in lively exercise, and to this end

will be much engaged in converse with God as he appears to the eye of faith in his glorious attributes, in his providential workings, and especially in his gracious manifestations through Christ and the Holy Spirit. He will be quick to mark the bearings of these upon his own experiences, and will try to hold his heart open to every address they make to it. Above all things he will prize the aid to be derived in this respect from secret prayer, social devotion and public worship.

3. He will seek to acquire an enlightened and active conscience, and in order to this will accustom himself to test his moral perceptions and judgments by the word of God, and to yield them assent and obedience on the ground of God's authority rather than because they seem to be right in his own eyes. A man may safely follow conscience when he consults it with a sincere desire to hear God speaking in its utterances, and when he requires it to verify its right to speak by harmonizing its utterances with the voice of God.

4. He will seek to preserve the purity

and the delicacy of his religious sensibilities, and in order to this will keep his affections fixed upon things which are really true and good and guard them against the seductive influence of those which are merely plausible and specious. He will "try the spirits" before he gives his faith to them. The chaste soul truly espoused to Christ will feel that in "calling evil good" in any form, or in "loving or making a lie," it is guilty both of treachery to its Lord and of defiling itself.

5. He will seek to abound in those charitable dispositions and works by which Jesus was so distinguished, and to this end will place himself in sympathy with the world around him and endeavor to keep his life mingling as a current of kindness with the common life of his generation.

6. He will seek, in a word, to reproduce in himself, so far as this is possible, the perfect mind and character of Christ, and to this end will by steady self-denial purge himself of his natural corruptions and faults, and with a patience and minuteness of attention like that of the sculptor will labor

to shape himself into a likeness to his Lord. It is thus by its onward motion that the religious life asserts its presence, as the clock serves the purpose of a clock only when its hands are traveling around the dial-plate. Therefore, says the apostle (Heb. xii. 1), "let us lay aside every weight and the sin that doth so easily beset us, and let us run with patience the race that is set before us, looking unto Jesus, the Author and Finisher of our faith."

IV.

The counterpart of what has just been said is that the Christian who wishes to grow in religion *will, as far as possible, disentangle himself* from all such associations and surroundings as are unfavorable to religion.

The Christian is the occupant of two spheres so intermingled that he must necessarily live in both. The one is the world, the other is the kingdom of God. It is his difficult duty to maintain the character of a subject of the kingdom of God while he is actually doing his part as a denizen of the world. It was with these contradictory elements of their condition in his view that the Saviour prayed for his disciples (John xvii. 15): "I pray not that thou shouldest take them out of the world, but that thou shouldest keep them from the evil." What the Saviour here prays the Father to do the honest professor of religion will himself endeavor to do—that is, keep himself from the evil to which he is exposed while in the world.

That there is evil in the world admits of no question. The policy of the world in its best forms is a policy which originates with the world and terminates upon the world. Directly it knows nothing of a God before, above or beyond the world. It never proposes to make men *religious*. It has no facilities to offer them in this direction. The religious man pursuing his aim as such will find himself in the position of a vessel beating its way by every device into port in the face of an opposing tide and contrary winds. The adverse power of the world does not so much lie in its gross forms of opposition to the kingdom of God as in that large class of occupations and enjoyments in which, it is said, a religious man may engage without ceasing to be religious. These occupations and enjoyments constitute a kind of common territory in which the Christian and the worldly man may meet. The policy of the world extends over it, or the worldly man would not be found there. Can the Christian enter it without being imbued with this policy? Can he consort there with men of the world without becoming like them, and so ceasing to be religious?

Here is the difficulty of his position; and hence the need of the counsel: Beware of these associations and surroundings, through which the policy of an irreligious world is operating, lest you be brought under the dominion of this policy. The voice that invites you into them is a siren voice. The evil against which the Saviour prayed lies lurking in them, and it becomes you to enter them with a cautious foot and to move among them with a vigilant eye.

No man, unless shielded and upheld by the grace of God, is proof against the power of these worldly associations and surroundings. His nature disposes him to accommodate himself to the element in which he is placed, and he cannot rely upon natural power, therefore, to protect him against the influence of that element. "Watch and pray lest ye enter into temptation," said the Lord to his disciples at a time when he foresaw that their natural strength was to be tried to the utmost by impending dangers. The cases are without number in the history of the people of God where men have started in their Christian course with the purest purposes and the warmest fervor, and afterward, by stepping too far into the stream of worldly business or pleasure, or by staying in it too long, have lost their steadfastness and have been swept away into all the excesses of a worldly life.

The Christian cannot go out of the world, but he is required not to be conformed to the world; and he must therefore guard himself against the transforming power of the world by keeping himself in contact and association with those patterns of life which belong to the kingdom of God. He must check the growing weight of the attractions of a worldly life by loading the opposite scale with a preponderating weight of spiritual interests and enjoyments. In the world he must appear as one abroad. In the fellowship of Christian minds, and in those scenes and occupations in which he may meet and converse with his Lord, he must find his home. O follower of Jesus, when you feel your relish for the exchange, the club-room or the haunts of social amusement exceeding and impairing your relish for the prayer-meeting, the religious conference or the society of your pious friends, be admonished that the pulse of spiritual life is declining, and that the danger of which your Master forewarned you under the name "the evil which is in the world" is becoming imminent in your case!

V.

The cultivation of religion will hardly be prosecuted unless *a deep sense of eternal things and an eternal world* is kept alive in the heart.

The "powers of the world to come" need to be set over against the powers of the world that now is. How constantly the disciples are stimulated to fidelity and watchfulness by references in the New Testament to the coming of the Lord! How earnestly the Christian racer is exhorted to keep his goal in view! How the fainting believer is rallied by the call to look away from the things which are seen and temporal to those which are not seen and eternal! It is the waiting for the Bridegroom that keeps the servant ready. The love of a world in which he naturally has so many interests, and with which he is so intimately associated, needs to be tempered for the Christian by cherishing aspirations after the higher one to which, as a joint-heir with Christ, he is destined; and the ardor with which treasure on earth is pursued must be moderated by a spiritual thrift which seeks to lay up treasure in heaven.

The traveler about to pass into a foreign country naturally anticipates the preparation required for his residence there and makes it beforehand. In the same way the Christian pilgrim will in all things aim to make his use of the present world subordinate to his well-being in the next. It is the man who habitually keeps his mind impressed with the transitory nature of the condition in which he is now placed, and forecasts the momentous state into which he is about to be introduced, who will be most likely to be found amidst all his worldly environments with his ear on the watch for the signal of departure and with his preparation for that event all complete. He will be most likely to avoid that "minding of the flesh" which is "enmity against God," and which hinders all spiritual growth, and to cultivate that "holiness without which no man can see the Lord." In the quaint words of the saintly Rutherford, "the instinct of nature maketh a man love his mother-country above all countries; the instinct of renewed nature and supernatural grace will lead you to such and such works—as to love your country above, to sigh to be clothed with your house not made with hands, and to call your borrowed prison here below a borrowed prison, and to look upon it servant-like and pilgrim-like; and the pilgrim eye and look is a disdainful-like, discontented cast of his eye, his heart crying after his eye, 'Fy! fy! This is not like my country!'"

VI.

It ought perhaps to be added, for the encouragement of the faithful Christian, that *growth in religion does not necessarily make itself known to the consciousness.* It may be going on where there is no sign which the subject of it can detect. Insensibly the child springs up into the man. Insensibly the true disciple advances in spiritual capacity and stature. He will never see the time when he will not need to struggle after further advancement. The larger the measure of his attainments, the higher will rise his ideal. He may seem not to be growing; but if the Spirit of God be in him, he is doing so. Despondency must not for a moment be entertained by the honest follower of Christ. Vigilance and exertion must never be relaxed. Infirmities may cling to him with an inveterate tenacity, besetting sins may show their vitality after years of repression, weakness or inadvertence may betray him into falls just when he is persuading himself he is most secure; but if from every failure and delinquency he rises with a more determined purpose to follow after Christ, that purpose is the sign of a life which is perhaps even growing more robust by overcoming the obstructions it encounters. The very effort to subdue corruption in one department of the soul may be the means of imperceptibly generating or developing grace in other departments. The evidence of progress in religion is to be found, not in the actual attainment of perfection, but in the patient and persevering effort to attain it. This is all the evidence that St. Paul had. "Brethren," he says (Phil. iii. 13), "I count not myself to have apprehended, but this one thing I do: forgetting those things which are behind, and reaching forth unto those things which are before, I press toward the mark for the prize of the high calling of God in Christ Jesus." And by the same evidence every Christian can assure himself of the same fact.

CHAPTER VII.

RELIGION IN THE CHURCH.

THE conduct of the church-member must in some way be affected by his union with the church.

This is to be expected; because, first, association or partnership always obliges a man to consult the will of his associates or partners; and, second, the church being an organization created for certain ends, each member of it is charged with an obligation to pursue those ends.

The man who after he has united with the church practically ignores the relation, and holds himself aloof from the corporate life and action of the church, is repeating the fallacy of the man who refuses to join the church on the ground that he can be as good a Christian out of the church as in it. In fact, he is adding inconsistency to unreasonableness and had better never have entered the church at all. Such inert members are a dead-weight upon the church rather than an accession to its force.

The followers of Christ constitute a household, and a household that has its distinct interests and duties. "All ye are brethren," said Christ (Matt. xxiii. 8), which means that every professed disciple of the Lord is bound to show himself a brother to his fellow-disciples. St. Paul, speaking of Christians, says (1 Cor. xii. 20), "Now are they many members, but one body." The "one body"—the church—has a life of its own which can be distinguished from the life of the several members, and yet is constituted by the united lives of the several members. The human body is a type of the church, composed of a diversity of members, so that each member is required in its acting to regard the well-being of the other members. The foot, for instance, must be governed in the use it makes of itself by a regard to the interests of the hand; and the eye, by a regard to the interests of the ear.

Besides, every church-member engages by a positive covenant to make the purposes for which the church exists his own. As it is the duty of every man who professes to be a follower of Christ to attach himself to his Church, so it is his duty—and a duty which he solemnly acknowledges by his connection with the church—to contribute his proportion of that efficiency which is required in order to enable the Church to execute the ministry which has been assigned to it by its divine Head. This ministry includes, first, certain offices to be performed to the body itself, and, second, certain offices to be performed to the world at large.

I.

In carrying out this ministry, evidently, every church-member should feel and express *a hearty interest in the affairs of the church.*

It is to be supposed that he had a definite motive in attaching himself to the Church and in soliciting membership in the particular church which he has joined. That motive should exhibit itself just as clearly in his subsequent conduct. What concerns the church, it should be henceforth seen, is a matter of personal concern to him.

It might seem supererogatory to give such counsel as this, and yet facts show that there is an occasion for it. Multitudes enter the Christian Church apparently without the least idea that they are thereby charging themselves with a specific set of corporate obligations. As in the matter of embracing Christ they were acting entirely in a private capacity, they are apt to carry the same feeling of isolation into the act of entering into the visible community of believers—an act which they regard as merely complementary to the other. Their solicitudes are therefore limited to themselves. They overlook the fact that in identifying themselves with this community they are identifying themselves with a living organism that gets its life and efficiency from the contributions of each constituent member.

Or if this fact is not entirely overlooked, the church-member may come to feel that he is fitted to occupy only a negative position in the church by reason of his low estimate of his personal abilities or his obscure social standing. The result is that such persons remain to a great extent strangers in the family into which they have been adopted. They are rather lodgers in the house of God than active members of the household. They are like the passengers of a ship, who, having been duly booked, feel that they have nothing to do but to sit quietly and be conveyed to their destination. They take it for granted that the seamen will attend to the management of the ship. This is to misread altogether the terms of their enlistment. They are the seamen, not the passengers; parties charged with the custody and conduct of a cargo, not representatives of that cargo. It was "not to be ministered unto, but to minister," that the Son of man came (Matt. xx. 28), and his followers must enter into his service and kingdom in the same spirit.

The actual exhibition of this spirit will depend upon the degree with which the professor of religion associates himself in interest and sympathy with the church to which he has attached himself. And, therefore, he needs to be admonished to see that his heart goes with his profession. "No man," said Jesus (Luke ix. 62), "having put his hand to the plough, and looking back"—or forgetting that his business is to drive the plough forward—" is fit for the kingdom of God." And as another consideration in favor of the duty I am enjoining it may be suggested that it is probable those who hold themselves aloof from church fellowship and church work will become complainers and unfriendly critics of what their brethren are doing. The men who do not plough are apt to occupy themselves with uncharitable faultfinding with the efforts of those who are attempting to plough, and so put themselves in the unenviable position of hinderers of the Lord's work.

II.

Every church-member is entrusted, to some degree, with the *maintaining of the character which the Church is intended, in the plan of its Founder, to illustrate.* He is to be the type, the living representative, of that "holy nation," that "peculiar people," which the followers of the Saviour are said to constitute.

In executing this trust he has a duty to perform first to his fellow-Christians. He is to exert such an influence as his circumstances and abilities allow in favor of that piety which is the characteristic of the spiritual family to which he belongs. He is to give light to others, as he in turn is to receive light from them. He may hold only a taper, and they a torch; but the taper can add to the light of the torch, or a taper brightly blazing may even replenish the waning light of an expiring torch. No man is without influence. By the power of example, if in no other way, he may affect others and contribute his share to the work of edifying the Church of God. No truly consistent, devout and godly church-member lives unnoticed or fails to quicken duller souls by the clear shining of his light.

Then, in the second place, there is an influence to be exerted in impressing the world with the divine specialty of the religion of Christ. Every church-member may be, and ought to be, an "epistle" of piety so legibly written that it may be "known and read of all men," and written, I may add, in such celestial characters that all men may be convinced that it is the product of the Holy Spirit. It is not the excellence of its creed nor of its government nor of its modes of worship which gives credit to a church in the eyes of worldly men. It is the exactness with which the members of a church fulfill the rigid practical tests which worldly men will be sure to apply to them. Inconsistent and irregular professors of religion, it is no exaggeration to say, are more effective enemies to the cause of Christ than the bitterest opponents to be found in the ranks of infidelity. What the Church ought to be as "the pillar and ground of the truth," and as the body of Christ animated by his Spirit, each particular Christian ought to be in his measure and sphere.

III.

It follows from this that every church-member ought to endeavor *to qualify himself for usefulness.*

A talent which has never been exercised

or called into practice places its possessor in a position not differing much from that of the man who, having received a talent, deliberately goes and hides it in a napkin. Two mites which a poor widow gave to the Lord were acknowledged by him. Every Christian probably has at his command a source of influence equivalent to these two mites. In fact, until the trial is honestly made, no one knows what gifts have been laid in his keeping. Poor as the distrustful disciple may deem himself, spiritually or intellectually, he can easily find some one else who is poorer, whose deficiencies can be supplied even out of his scanty resources.

The art of being useful, like all other arts, is to be acquired by practice. No man knows the ability there is in him till, like the spark struck from the steel, it has been brought out by the stroke of effort. In the different departments of religious work laid out for itself by any active church, such as Sabbath- and mission-schools, prayer-meetings, benevolent associations and evangelical visitation and labor, an opportunity is offered for the use of every kind of talent;

and every kind of talent is usually welcomed by those who superintend these departments. At all events, the home and the family form a sphere in which the humblest individual may do good.

Particularly I would suggest that the prayer-meeting—which is eminently a social institution where Christians seek to be helpers of one another's faith and joy—lays a special claim upon the male members of a church. A meeting for prayer implies, of course, that among the parties present there are some who are able and willing to offer prayer. It is not said that all present are under an obligation to do this, for it is evident that the gifts which qualify a person profitably to lead the minds of others in this exercise are not indiscriminately granted to all Christians. But it is just as evident that if the prayer-meeting is to be sustained, an obligation rests upon some—and upon a sufficient number—of a congregation to see that this duty is performed. The question, therefore, ought to press itself upon the mind of every conscientious church-member, "Can I not in this way serve the church?"

The reluctance which is naturally felt to the performance of a public service like this is not a sufficient reason for concluding that the obligation does not exist, for many a duty has to be performed at the cost of self-denial. Where the voice of the church distinctly calls for the rendering of such a service at the hands of any of its members, it is probably safe to conclude that it is their duty to render it; and it is equally safe to expect that the grace which is promised to all believers in every time of need will upon trial successfully carry them through all the difficulties which beset it.

The man who is accustomed to offer prayer to God in secret and in audible words, as it is—at least sometimes—well to do, and who in addition conducts worship in his family, as all Christian householders ought to do, will find that he has at hand all the subjects and all the phrases which are needed at the prayer-meeting. The ambition which aims at making a *fine* prayer is not only out of place on such an occasion, but ought to be repressed as a positive offence against God. The social prayer is generally most seasonable and effective when it is simple and short. Considering the benefit which may be communicated to pious souls through the medium of a prayer offered by another—a benefit which every Christian has experienced—the ability to pray for and with others is surely a talent which ought to be coveted.

The predicament in which a professedly religious man finds himself when the request is made to him by some suffering or dying fellow-being, "Pray for me," and the reply has to be given, "I cannot," is a sad one. It is one which has often occurred. Surely it is one which ought never to have occurred. The follower of Christ ought to be as ready to respond to the appeal "Pray for me" as his Master was to give an answer to his disciples' request, "Lord, teach us to pray."

IV.

The church-member should be a coadjutor with his brethren in every *authorized effort to support and propagate Christianity.*

The church which can hear the Lord say, "Go ye into all the world and preach the gospel to every creature" (Mark xvi. 15), and yet refuse to engage in such efforts, is like the son who to his father's command, "Go work to-day in my vineyard," replied, "I will not" (Matt. xxi. 28). It is belieing its character as a church.

Now, a church is an organized body and does its work in an orderly and regular way. It is under a divinely-constituted government. It is the duty of the governing officers to see that the church is prosecuting its appropriate benevolent and evangelical labors, and it is to be presumed that these officers, from their position and from the directness of their responsibility, will be best able to define the kind of labors in which the body of Christ's followers ought at any time to engage. The faithful church-member will therefore accord to the governing powers of his church an authority to direct him in this matter. He will accept the system of operations devised by his church for its members as a good one, and will feel himself under obligation to yield it his support unless a clear conviction of his duty to God constrains him to do otherwise.

The position that church-authorities have no right to prescribe to the private member his duty in this respect, and that he may lawfully withhold his support from any church enterprise because he does not see the expediency of it or because he does not deem it as important as some other enterprise, is undoubtedly a wrong one. Church-members who, for instance, oppose missions among the heathen, as some do, on these grounds, although the judgment of the deliberative and governing authorities of the church has unanimously pronounced the work to be effected by such missions to be one which Christian people cannot overlook without expressing disloyalty to their Lord, are failing to acknowledge as they ought to do the authority of those who are appointed to rule over and admonish them. A certain amount of obedience to those who are charged with the oversight of the house of God is due from those who have come under the household law.

Such schemes of benevolent and evangelistic work as have been devised by the church will be adopted by every well-disposed church-member as an object of personal interest and sustained to the best of his ability. In fact, these schemes are methods devised for him and facilities furnished to him by the church for the doing of his own private work. They are not to be looked upon as an imposition. They create no new obligation, but are rather helps to the Christian in discharging an obligation already existing. A poor-fund in the church, under the management of the deacons, only gives him the opportunity, through what he contributes to it, of more easily reaching the poor, whom as a follower of Christ he was already under an obligation to relieve. The Board or the committee of Domestic Missions to which he is occasionally asked to make a contribution is only an intermediate agent proposing to aid him in doing a part which is already incumbent on him in the work of sending the gospel to the destitute.

It follows from this that every church-member ought to place giving to religious objects alongside of praying or communing at the Lord's table in his scheme of religious living. The church is required to present to God the spectacle of a people "zealous of good works" just as distinctly as it is required to present to him that of a people zealous for devotional rites or sacramental solemnities. All the elements which belong to the principle of piety—such as faith, love, gratitude, zeal for God's honor, and so on—are brought into exercise in the act of religious giving as truly as in acts of worship. For this reason this act is properly admitted among the forms of worship practiced in the public devotions of the Sabbath, and every worshiper should feel the same obligation to join in it that he feels to take part in the prayers and the psalms.

It is noticeable with what explicitness the Scriptures give directions as to the performance of this act of worship. Thus, they teach, *first*, that it is to be performed with a willing mind: "God loveth a cheerful giver" (2 Cor. ix. 7); *second*, that it is to be performed with a pure desire to honor God and without any stinting as to measure: "He that giveth let him do it with simplicity" (Rom. xii. 8); *third*, that the offering is to bear a proportion to each individual's ability: "Let every one of you lay by him in store as God hath prospered him" (1 Cor. xvi. 2); and *fourth*, that it should be performed as a continuous and systematic exercise, and be provided for in advance of special occasions by every man's setting apart "on the first day of the week" or at regular times a portion of his means for religious uses. Such giving, if universally practiced, would furnish the church with the ability to carry forward all its enterprises, and would return a hundred-fold blessing to the souls of those concerned in it.

V.

It is clear from this statement of his duties that the church-member needs to *keep himself informed* in regard to much that belongs to the economic life of the church.

The ignorance which prevails amongst the professed followers of the Lord in reference to many things which are fundamental to their right religious living is deplorable. It may not be possible for every member of a church to know everything which it would be profitable for him to know, but it certainly is desirable that every one should possess himself of all the knowledge which is requisite to give consistency and symmetry to his Christian walk. He should know enough of the constitution of his church to be satisfied that it rests upon a good scriptural and historical warrant, and on this account mainly should conscientiously adhere to it. He should know enough of its system of doctrine, and of the correspondence of this with the word of God, to be enabled intelligently to accept it. He should know enough of its organic structure to understand the names and the functions of its various officers and courts and to follow it in the working of its different departments. He should take an interest in the proceedings of church-councils. He should acquaint himself with the outlying field in which the church is called to work, and with the nature and progress of the work which the church is actually doing in that field. He should know what every church agency he is asked to support means, why it has been called into existence and why it claims his support.

To acquire this knowledge, even in a moderate degree, will of course demand some effort in the way of reading and research. Especially it will require the aid of the religious periodical. The history of the Church from year to year—almost from week to week—is stamped now upon the pages of the religious newspaper and magazine and spread before the eyes of the world. It is so important a record that no honest Christian can consent to be ignorant of it; it is so accessible that there is hardly any one who cannot afford to possess himself of it. Every church-member should be the reader of a Church paper, and perhaps it is not too much to say that every church should make provision for supplying with such a paper every member who is too poor to subscribe for one.

VI.

It may now be added that, apart from his duty as a pious man to worship God, it is incumbent on the member of a church, as a part of the duty which he owes to his fellow-Christians and the community around him, *to be punctual and regular in his attendance upon public worship.*

"Not forsaking the assembling of ourselves together" is associated (Heb. x. 25) with the duty of "considering one another and provoking unto love and good works." The bond of sympathy is weakened, the community of interest is abated, in any congregation, by the withdrawal of the countenance and support of any of its members. Each heart is kindled into a warmer glow by the presence and the co-operation of another heart that beats in unison with itself, and the lack of heartiness which is manifested by the professed friends of religion when they fail to appreciate and join in the assemblies of their brethren operates just as decidedly in chilling the heartiness of those who are thus abandoned. Minister and people alike feel aggrieved by such an exhibition of disaffection.

When the professed friends of religion can so lightly esteem its ordinances, what must be the effect upon the minds of those who are naturally inclined to deny their authority? When such discrediting of the institutions of Christianity is witnessed among its avowed adherents, what can be expected but an emboldened opposition to them on the part of the worldly-minded, and a general rush of the community into Sabbath desecration and every other form of popular irreligion?

The altars of God are the bulwarks of virtue and morality as well as of piety, and it is the saddest of all sights to see the hands of the followers of Jesus concerned in laying them waste. Surely the woe denounced by the Saviour upon the man by whom an offence cometh will hang over the head of the disciple who so discourages the hearts of his fellow-believers, and so lends his endorsement to the profane multitude who say of Zion, "Rase it, rase it, even to the foundation thereof!"

CHAPTER VIII.

RELIGION IN SECULAR LIFE.

IMPORTANT as is religion in the Church, it is, if possible, more important outside of the Church.

It is probable that piety in the soul of a Christian is cultivated and developed as much by the hard exercise he has to undergo in the world as it is by the observance of the ordinances of the Church, just as the musician is made by painstaking practice as much as by the study of theoretical principles. And when we take into view the further duty of the Christian to impress the minds of worldly persons with the reality and the excellency of religion as a governing principle in a man's life, the power must be drawn almost entirely from the evidences which are to be found in his practical deportment.

Worldly men will naturally discredit the claim of any man to be a true Christian who does not show his religion on the plane of his worldly life. And the Christian should take no exception to this test. For religion, being a property of the soul or an abiding element in the man himself, must be expected to evince its presence wherever the man appears and in everything that he does. In the nature of it, it is a permanent, not an intermittent, force. It will demonstrate itself like the steady shining of the diamond, not like the transient sparkle of the dewdrop. It must exhibit its power in all the circumstances, and over all the circumstances, of a man's life, in order to show that it is in itself something more than a mere circumstance. It must reveal itself in the gait of a man's daily walk, and not be assumed on set occasions, like the soldier's measured step on parade.

Further, it is to be considered that by far the greater part of every man's time is necessarily employed in secular occupations. It would be a singular incongruity if a supreme interest like religion were to find a place in which to assert its claims or to enforce its authority only in the minimum of a man's life. That which is enjoined upon men as their first and highest duty cannot certainly be thrust away into a fraction of the week, so as to be excluded from the work of six days and confined to the formal exercises of the Sabbath. And, what is of more importance still, it is on the field of the world that religion is put to its severest trials and is required to give the best proof of its celestial origin and temper. Till it has shown itself competent to maintain its ground on this field it cannot demand the confidence of worldly men. It cannot be stronger than its weakest part. It must betray no weak part on that side which is especially exposed to the scrutiny of worldly men. If it does, the whole fabric of its pretensions falls. Therefore, said the Saviour (Matt. v. 16), "let your light so shine before men that they may see your good works and glorify your Father which is in heaven."

The divine lustre of religion must be made to shine "before men" by being exhibited where men resort or in the public thoroughfares and market-places. It must indicate its presence and power by producing "good works" or works which glorify God on a soil where such works are not naturally found, or it will fail to fulfill the function which the Author of it has assigned to it. "The true light which lighteth every man that cometh into the world" is actually to accomplish that which in its nature it is adapted to do through the shining of the followers of Christ. The darkness of the world is to be dispelled not merely by the teaching of the preacher or by the argument of the polemic, but by the practical demonstration of the sanctifying power of religion afforded by the living luminary—the upright and consistent Christian.

What a distinguished Scotch divine has said in closing a paper upon modern agnosticism is true of all the forms of unbelief current in the world: "The strongest of all anti-agnostic forces—in fact, the one great safeguard of humanity against the general or final triumph of agnosticism—is none other than the redemptive power of the glorious gospel of Jesus Christ. Each one of you—fathers, brothers, sisters—by simply so living as to show that religion is supremely worth believing, may do far more to combat the spirit whence agnosticism arises than I or any one could do by a merely formal written attack upon it. The grand argument against anti-religious agnosticism is the practical one of a consistent and vigorous Christian life—the argument which, through God's grace, we can all use."

I.

In carrying his religion into secular life, the Christian is to be careful that it gets, through his representation of it, *a fair showing before the eye of the world.*

This Christ asks of his followers, and it is all that he asks. He does not expect them to improve upon his doctrines or regulations, but he does expect them to give to these a just setting forth in their character and their conduct. The style of manhood which is depicted by our Lord and his apostles in their teachings is unquestionably amiable and beautiful. In assuming it human nature is embellished with every genuine virtue which can attach to it. When the counsel is given, therefore, in Tit. ii. 10, that believers should "adorn the doctrine of God their Saviour in all things," the meaning is, not that they should by any devices of their own strive to make this doctrine attractive, but that they should allow it, through them as its medium, to make a clear and full exhibition of the attractiveness which intrinsically belongs to it.

God's image in the soul is certainly a perfect thing. The study of the Christian must be to express that image faultlessly, and to keep it from being obscured or marred by infirmities of his own. Whatever deforms character, as coarseness of manner, untidiness of habit, vulgarity in speech, irritability of temper or ill-breeding in any form, is at variance with the spirit of the gospel, and can never appear in a professor of religion without in some degree doing damage to the credit of religion. The morbid distempers and the offensive obliquities to which a man may be naturally disposed or to which he has become addicted are in the case of the Christian more than blemishes in the man: they are so many blots on the good name of Christianity, and will be noted by the enemies of religion as so many evidences of its being a pretension rather than a divine power in the soul. The censorious eyes of the world are at all times upon the follower of Christ, and a merciless rigor of judgment will be applied by it to his most trivial acts. It becomes him, therefore, to remember the ordeal to which he is exposed and in every phase of his life and conduct, jealously to maintain "a good report with them which are without."

If religion does not improve the nature of a man, it will have to bear, at the bar of public opinion, the reproach of all the faults which adhere to it. The crooked limb may have been in the vine originally; but if religion does not prune it off, religion will be charged with its existence. Hence the Scriptures descend to such minuteness in portraying the Christian life as to denounce such characters as the "busybody" and the "brawler," and to forbid such things as "filthiness," "foolish talking" and "jesting" as things "which are not convenient"—that is, not suitable to the Christian. "Be pitiful," "Be gentle," "Be courteous," are counsels which they continually reiterate. Religion is a refiner's fire in reference to the outward man as well as to the inward. St. Paul has brought honor to Christianity by his delicate sensibility and his gentlemanly bearing, as well as by the breadth and power of his expositions of truth. The separateness from the world which the gospel enjoins does not mean the abandonment of the decencies of life nor the amenities of society, and no follower of Christ can disregard them in his intercourse with his fellow-men without injuring the religion which he represents in the same way and to the same extent as "dead flies" are said (Eccl. x. 1) to corrupt "the ointment of the apothecary."

II.

To this suggestion it ought to be added that religion is *not to be recommended to the world by any ostentatious modes of demonstration.*

The man who is seeking to advertise himself or get credit to himself as a professor of religion, is sacrificing the honor of religion in order to honor himself. Unseasonably introduced or offensively obtruded, religion fails to command the respect which the follower of Christ should always aim to draw to it. Sincerity, consistency and good sense are what the shrewd men of the world expect to find in a Christian, and what they have a right to expect. These forbid the use of any factitious methods or any appearance of study or any resort to the arts of display in the practice of religion. Any peculiarity which gives a man the air of one playing a part will awaken a suspicion as to his integrity, and in the case of religion will give occasion to its adversaries to brand the system itself as an imposture. It is by depicting so-called religious characters under this form—as thrusting their piety forward in grotesque and unseemly ways, or as hanging out the badges of their religion in circumstances in which these have no place, or as indulging in unreal cant—that some of the writers of popular literature have sought to bring religion generally into discredit and contempt.

The truly religious man will act religiously, if I may so express it, without thinking of what he is doing, or at least without giving the public any advertisement of the fact. He will be simply himself; which is to be the religious man. Except on special occasions, it will be by indirect rather than by direct methods that he will affirm his religion. In performing an act of faith he will not sound a trumpet before him, as the hypocrites do. He will do it because his thought is on God, who seeth in secret, not on himself or his fellow-man. He will strive to please all men so far as he can do this consistently with fidelity to God; and when he has to offend any, he will do it in such a way as obliges them to see that he cannot please them without offending God.

III.

Men of the world will always put facts before theories or professions. The Christian *must offer facts in verification of his claim* to be a religious man.

On the stage of secular life these must be facts of a secular sort. In regard to the great majority of men, their secular occupations are made up of the handling and making of money, and in their case the use of money becomes the index of character. The desire for money, as every one knows, is apt to become an inordinate passion, blighting the more generous affections of the soul and converting the man into the mere cold lover of self. Every one knows, too, that the mere accumulation of money is in itself a childish, not to say ignoble, end for a rational being to set before him. The love of money in its grossest form makes the miser, and the miser is universally regarded as a despicable character. The spirit of the miser is in every man who makes money-getting, without regard to the use of it, the supreme object of his life and the supreme source of his enjoyment. That spirit even the world brands as disloyalty to the better instincts of human nature. How much more flagrantly must it appear in the case of the Christian to be disloyal to God!

The professor of religion is bound, therefore, to throw into his pursuit of wealth a moderation of temper which the policy of the world does not require. Though standing side by side with the mere money-getter in this pursuit, he must show that he is animated by a different motive, and that his love to God is a stronger principle than his desire for money. His position as a party to this pursuit is not wrong. Occupation is one of the conditions of man's well-being, and occupation aims at results which are conveniently represented by money. It is right for the religious man to seek wealth, but not simply for wealth's sake. In its proper place it is a means for satisfying his needs, gratifying his wholesome tastes and enlarging his capacity for serving God by serving his generation. It would seem to be a reasonable proposition that a man's desire for money ought to be regulated and limited by his desire for that which money enables him to do, and that when this latter desire has been fully provided for the former one ought to cease to operate.

Would it not be a strong illustration of the power of religious principle if the Christian were some time to be seen stopping in his pursuit of wealth and saying, "I have enough," and devoting the residue of his life, as a sort of Sabbath-resting after his toils, to such occupations as directly minister to the cause of benevolence and religion? The Church needs just such men of opulence and leisure to fill its offices, and the world wants them to carry on its schemes of reform and charity.

Or if an escape from the habits and the implications of business be an impossibility, what is to hinder the religious man to whom God has given enough for all his own wants from making God, if I may so express it, a partner in his future operations and prosecuting his business and gathering in his gains in the interest of God and for the furtherance of his kingdom? Instances have occurred where men have so made themselves literally the stewards of God, illustriously showing that riches, which the

Saviour declared to be so generally a fatal bar in the path to heaven, may be converted into the golden stairway which leads the possessor directly into it.

If cupidity of disposition is to be avoided by the Christian, I may now remark more emphatically, All dishonesty in practice is to be avoided by him. The world never forgives an act of fraud, and, we may say, never *forgets* it. A pecuniary loss inflicted on one man by another is a wrong which rankles longest in the memory of the injured party and is the hardest to be condoned by the offender. On this account the professor of religion should look upon the contracting of a debt as an act which brings him into fearful proximity to the region of possible dishonesty. The imperiling of the rights of others by any presumptuous adventure in business, or a resort to equivocal measures to escape a just obligation to others, or a complicity in any of the other thousand forms of loose practice or sharp practice which are current in the world, should be repelled from his thought by the follower of Christ as promptly as his Master repelled the suggestion of the devil that he should cast himself from the pinnacle of the temple in the expectation that the angels would protect him from harm.

The religion of Christ has no more effective enemy than is to be found in the person of the professor who has suffered his name to become blackened with an imputation of dishonesty. The Church is everywhere bleeding from the wounds inflicted by its false or heedless members who have been betrayed into wrong-doing by their intemperate lust for gain.

IV.

Afflictions, troubles and disappointments fill so large a part of the ordinary life of men that they constitute a common ground upon which the Christian and the man of the world may meet and compare their principles. It is to be expected that religion will show its power by affording to the possessor of it some advantage which the irreligious man does not possess under the pressure of these painful experiences.

Apart from religion there are no resources accessible to men in their times of adversity but such as are found in fortitude or the passive acceptance of the inevitable, in the diversion of mind afforded by occupation, in the promises of hope or in the soothing influences of time. These are as open to the Christian as they are to others, but in his case faith supplies additional and immeasurably superior solaces and supports.

It does not promise him exemption from the tribulations which are common to all men, but it does profess to give him a mastery over the tribulations of the world to which men naturally cannot attain. Men of the world have, therefore, a right to watch the deportment of the Christian under the discipline of sorrow, and to demand from him in the trying exigences of life the evidence of a power in his principles to sustain him of which they, in their lack of faith, are destitute.

Much may be done for the honor of Christ by his followers in such testing-times by maintaining a temper and a demeanor in harmony with the doctrines and the promises of the gospel. The pain which accompanies misfortune in any form, the anguish of a bereaved heart or the stunning effect of a commercial catastrophe are experiences which irreligious men understand as well as religious ones, and any advantage possessed by the latter in these circumstances is something which the former are capable of appreciating. It is a good time, therefore, to glorify God before an unbelieving world when the believer is "in the fires." It is his privilege as well as his duty so to conduct himself under the reverses of life that his neighbors shall see that a divine Comforter is with him in the furnace.

The annals of the Church, from the times of the apostles down, are full of testimonials to the power of religion to brace the soul with courage in the face of dangers before which nature quails, and to make it patient under sufferings against which nature revolts; but each generation and each community calls for daily living attestations of this power to meet the daily living skepticism of the world. Each follower of Christ, in passing through his own "valley of weeping," should be ready to give such testimony to the abiding faithfulness and the sufficient grace of his Lord. To be able to give it when the demand for it arises which may come suddenly, it is necessary the Christian should habitually live in near fellowship with God. It is when the eye has been familiar with Christ by day that the hand can find him in the darkness of the night. It is the heart that has carried in it the essence of faith and love in its sound state that will, when broken by adversity,

> "like the plants that throw
> Their fragrance from the wounded part,
> Breathe sweetness out of woe."

V.

It is equally incumbent on the Christian to prove to the world that in virtue of his religion he is *superior to the deteriorating influences of prosperity.*

These influences are perhaps even more dangerous to a Christian's steadfastness than are those of adversity. To be in possession of that which worldly men worship with an idolatrous love, and yet to keep himself free from this idolatrous love, is the hard task set before the wealthy follower of Christ. It is the exhibition of a radical distinction between him and worldly men which the latter are bound to notice. It is like the proof of his religious principle which Daniel gave when he turned away from the provision of the king's meat and wine which was offered him and chose to subsist upon pulse and water. To keep this proof always clearly revealed to the eyes of his fellow-men in his daily intercourse with them is the duty of the religious man, and it is a duty which should remind him that if he needs divine grace to keep him from fault in the acquisition of wealth he needs it just as much to enable him to maintain his integrity in the use of it.

There are two obvious ways in which prosperity may lead the Christian into a departure from his principles. The first grows out of the fact that wealth gives importance to the possessor of it. The natural result of this fact is that he should become inflated with a *sense* of his importance. The second follows upon the other fact—that wealth presents to the possessor of it the means of indefinite indulgence. The natural effect of this fact is to excite *love* of indulgence. A sense of one's importance is, of course, a magnifying of self; and as self engrosses the contemplation of the mind other objects recede, until all affinity with them is lost sight of and the man withdraws into a condition of cold isolation.

Let the prosperous Christian guard against this natural propensity. Let him show that wealth has not blunted or contracted his sympathy with his kind, and that his heart has not become encased in the gold which his hands have gathered. The follower of Christ must exhibit before the world the grand spectacle of a man who, while he is lifted by his riches above participation in the wants of the multitudes below him, still cherishes with special care the Christian charities which make these wants an object of personal interest. The other danger—that of an excessive devotion to the indulgences which wealth places within the reach of its possessor—is one which the Christian needs perhaps still more carefully to avoid.

This duty leads us to a consideration of the difficult and delicate question, How far may the professor of religion indulge, without detriment to his own spiritual well-being and the honor of religion, in what are designated by the comprehensive term "worldly amusements"? This question is one which, in a pleasure-loving age like the present, is sure to force itself upon the attention of every one embarking in a religious life. It seems entirely reasonable to say that in order that a Christian may lawfully indulge in these amusements it is necessary that he should be well assured that in doing so he is not breaking down that line of separation which he is required always to make manifest between himself and the mere man of the world. In determining this point it may aid him to reflect upon the following facts.

First. That the very prevalent argument that because religion was designed to make people cheerful and happy, and because worldly amusements are expressly employed to produce this effect, therefore religious people may properly indulge in these amusements, is a fallacy. It forgets that the Christian religion defines cheerfulness and happiness at the same time that it sanctions them. It does not resign its authority when it approaches the realms of pleasure. Here, as in all other departments of conduct, it has some limits to fix and some distinctions to draw. Its law prescribes the ways in which men are to be cheerful and happy, as well as all their other ways of acting. When it invites them to rejoice, it surely does not send them to an ungodly world to learn how they are to rejoice. The follower of Christ is bound to follow him—that is, to follow his direction—as much in his amusements as in anything else. Christ has never given authority to society to direct his followers. By a certain portion of society the bacchanalian revel and the excitement of the gaming-table are regarded as sources of cheerfulness and happiness. Is it to be supposed that Christ would bid his followers take part in these amusements? Who will say so?

Second. That the plea—which is also very frequently urged—that what everybody does it must be right for the Christian to do, since it cannot be required of him to make himself singular or to banish himself from society, is equally fallacious. This argument will be a good one when everybody studies in everything to follow Christ. But surely it cannot be a safe rule for the Christian to do as the community does when that community, to a large extent, openly denies Christ and repudiates his right to control and guide it. The Christian's rule clearly requires him distinctively to differ from such a community.

Third. That worldly amusements, in the well-understood sense of that term, mean forms of pleasure which have been invented by the world. They are not home-born to the Christian, but are imported from a foreign soil. They do not belong even to that general economy under which God in his goodness has spread out, as it were, a banquet for all his children to enjoy.

They are something which the cravings of men have superadded to that banquet. They are the product of a worldly mind, suited to a worldly taste. The agents who have originated them and who preside over them are not the representatives of the kingdom of God.

The radical difference between the Christian and the votary of these worldly amusements appears in this—that there can be no reciprocity in their enjoyments. In his association with the worldly man in his amusements the Christian makes a concession which the worldly man will not reciprocate. The former is expected to affiliate with the latter, but the latter never affiliates with the former. No one would dream of seeing a frequenter of the theatre or of the race-course going with the Christian neighbor who had been induced to accompany him to those places of amusement to attend the prayer-meeting or the religious assembly which that neighbor must be supposed to love to attend. The professor of religion must drop his distinctive character just in the measure that he identifies himself with those who are so alien to him in disposition and in taste. He must become like those who cannot become like him; which is certainly very much the same thing as ceasing to act as a Christian.

The primitive Christians had been accustomed, many of them, in their unconverted days, to attend the gladiatorial shows in which men slaughtered one another for the entertainment of the spectators. These shows formed one of the worldly amusements of the age. They had been invented to give pleasure to a brutal appetite. When converted, these Christians knew that this amusement had never been sanctioned by their divine Master, and knew that in countenancing it they were compromising their character as followers of Christ and throwing themselves into the ranks of his enemies. They abandoned them, and it is said that through their opposition the barbarous sport was finally abolished.

Fourth. That worldly amusements are *extreme* forms in which the love of pleasure seeks to gratify itself. They are intemperate indulgences, as distinguished from temperate ones. Now, intemperance or a tendency to go to an extreme in the gratification of one's appetites is an evidence of a derangement in nature. It shows that what ought to be a wholesome craving for pleasure has become a feverish thirst. The world says that this thirst must be satisfied, and invents pleasures for the purpose of satisfying it. Religion says that this tendency of a deranged nature must be resisted. It opposes the law of moderation to the law of excess. As has been stated in a former paragraph, the Christian is required, even in the indulgence of sorrow, to put limits to the expression of his grief, and to avoid the extremes of despondency and woe. And shall not religion equally set bounds to his hilarity? Can he lawfully run to the extremes to which nature would lead him in this direction when he is forbidden to do so in the other? Surely the conscientious Christian ought to feel debarred from following an unbelieving world into the regions of pleasure by the same principle which restrains him from abandoning himself, as nature leads worldly men to do, to the sway of a hopeless sorrow. Self-denial in either case is demanded of the follower of Christ for Christ's sake.

Fifth. That the character of worldly amusements is to be estimated very much by the concomitants which they gather around them.

In its simple form an amusement may be admitted to be innocent, and yet, from the incidents which are invariably associated with it, may be altogether objectionable. This test is particularly applicable to the theatre. "What greater harm," it is often asked, "can there be in seeing the drama of *Hamlet* personated on the stage by gifted actors than in reading it in Shakespeare's works?" Could the former exercise be kept free from corrupting adjuncts, as the latter is, the answer might be "No greater." The Christian may read *Hamlet* as an intellectual entertainment without detriment to his religious state. The exhibition of *Hamlet* on the stage, however, is given for the purpose of deriving a pecuniary profit from the attendance of the public. The public indiscriminately must be attracted. The species of the attraction employed is a secondary matter provided the end can be reached—that of drawing together a paying crowd. Mere intellectual gratification would not seem to be sufficient to secure on a large enough scale the desired attendance, and therefore attractions of other sorts—some of them unquestionably of a vicious tendency—must be associated with the exhibition.

Friendly to virtue as the advocates of the playhouse would make it, they must admit that in the adjuncts which seem to be inseparable from it it is utterly demoralizing. The same test should be applied to the solution of the question as to the right of the professor of religion to engage in the fashionable dance and the dancing-party.

This is a question which will almost certainly demand the consideration of the young Christian. Granting that in itself dancing is a harmless exercise, and that in its simpler forms social dancing does not differ from other recreations in which both sexes participate, it may still on good grounds be urged that the concomitants which have become attached to it in ordinary practice have placed it in that category of dissipated and extravagant pleasures in which the religious man cannot consistently indulge. As society employs and patronizes it—as a cultivated and elaborate art, as an occupation involving a necessity for ostentatious dressing, for luxurious festivity, for promiscuous association, for the consumption of time in preparation for and recovery from the period of revelry and for risk to bodily health; as an amusement carrying along with it all the adjuncts of the modern ball—through its surroundings, dancing has become an entertainment so essentially worldly that the Christian must apparently take leave of his distinctive character in taking part in it. It is a wise rule in regard to customs as well as men to judge them by the company they keep.

Sixth. That the enjoyment derived from these worldly amusements is purchased at an immense cost. This cost appears in the loss which the pursuit of them entails of a capacity to relish other enjoyments. False appetites or those which have been forced upon nature are stronger than those which originally belong to nature, and in proportion as they are indulged blunt and enfeeble the latter. Devotion to novel-reading thus unfits a person to relish soberer and sounder literature. The Christian who suffers his heart to come under the fascinations of worldly pleasure will dearly pay for the license he has allowed himself. From the numbness which these will infuse into his higher spiritual nature, he will find himself disqualified in a large measure for pure intellectual enjoyment, and in a still larger measure for the enjoyment of the peculiar pleasures which religion offers to the genuine living believer. His deadened sensibilities will no more respond to the promptings of the Holy Spirit, devout meditation will become a weariness, prayer will decline into a heartless form, and the Scriptures will cease to be vocal with the messages of God.

The conclusion to which a fair inspection of these worldly amusements would lead a dispassionate mind would seem to be this —that the follower of Christ is required, under the most favorable view he can take of them, to lay down the rule, "I will indulge in them with strict moderation, or within such bounds as may be compatible with my spiritual well-being;" and if, upon experiment, he finds that moderation is impossible in the case, or that even with it these worldly amusements are unfriendly to his religious comfort and progress, he ought to say, "I will altogether refrain from indulging in them." Probably it is just here on this ground, where the world is addressing its most plausible and seductive solicitations to the Church, that the dividing-line between the Church and the world needs to be most sharply drawn.

CHAPTER IX.

RELIGION IN THE FAMILY.

SO much of the real, genuine life of a man is brought into exercise and into light in the sphere of the family that perhaps it would not be extravagant to say that this sphere is the crucial one for the follower of Christ.

If a man be a religious man, he will certainly demonstrate the fact at home. If there he fails to exemplify that character, he leaves all other evidences of it, to say the least, open to suspicion.

The family was the first sanctuary in which religion had a visible birth and in which it took form and voice—the shrine from which divine oracles addressed the soul in advance of the prophets' inspired utterances. In its very organization—in the relations it creates and the offices it institutes—it seems to be an earthly pattern of a heavenly economy or kingdom which God has been pleased to designate as his "house," and in which he appears as presiding as Head over all the inmates and gathering them under his wings as his children. The typology of the family is so religious that if religion be absent from it, it seems as if its essential element were wanting. The fact of God's fatherhood toward men is mirrored in every spectacle of a human parent looking down with loving watchfulness upon his little household flock, and the reciprocal obligation on the part of men to acknowledge this fatherhood is symbolized wherever the flock is seen looking up with trusting eyes to the parent's guardian care.

The interests of the home-life, too, are of such a nature as to make it almost indispensable that God should be acknowledged and depended upon by the family. They impose upon each member the charge of the well-being of every other member—a charge which in the exercise of it involves an indefinite amount of the tenderest solicitude and calls for a measure of power and wisdom which transcends the resources of man. A family without God in it is in a condition like that of the household from which the literal head is absent. At every turn it is reminded of its need of his presence. It is painfully incomplete without him. In the world men may do without God; they cannot do without him at home. Things which may be divorced from him as they are regarded in the place of business are necessarily associated with him when surveyed in the atmosphere of home-life. Bankruptcy means loss of property on the exchange; it means the loss of bread in the presence of wife and children. The fear of it in the former place stimulates to exertion; in the latter it extorts the prayer, "Give us this day our daily bread." Sickness and death may occur in the community around us, and we accept them as the inevitable results of the law of nature. They enter our doors, and, though it be an infant who is the victim, every hand is raised, as it were, in resistance, and every voice invokes the aid of a power above nature and cries, "God be merciful to the child!"

Nowhere does God touch us so closely or make us so conscious of our dependence upon him as in the sphere of these home-interests, and nowhere, probably, outside of his Bible, can the Christian find a volume so adapted to foster and train his religious sentiments and principles as that which he may find in his home-experiences.

And surely, I may add, if the desire to win others to Christ be a natural feature in the mind of a true believer, he will be constrained to evince it most conspicuously in his intercourse with those who are loved by him as he loves his own soul. If a man's religion is to be a light anywhere, ought it not to be such at the central point of his world, and in that little domestic circle with which his life is naturally bound up? The force of the obligation to make a faithful, and at the same time an attractive, exhibition of piety here is simply incalculable. This consideration is sustained by the further thought that if a Christian in his family is not making an impression favorable to religion, he is in all likelihood doing a positive injury to it. The home is the spot where the sharpest possible scrutiny is always directed to the walk of the professed follower of Christ. The eyes of children are watchful organs, and keen as they are watchful, and their minds are prompt to form judgments upon what they see. Instinctively they put confidence in a parent, and love to bestow that confidence without limit. It is a sad discovery which is made when it is found that that confidence has been misplaced—when a child is forced to conclude, through the faults or the inconsistencies observed in a parent, that his religion is not what it professes to be. And it is as disastrous as it is sad, for it shakes the confidence of the child in truth itself. What can be confided in when a parent has proved false? Perhaps, if the matter were closely sifted, it would be found that the actual deviations from rectitude which the younger members of a family see in the conduct of their seniors constitute the reason why they are so frequently unaffected by the instructions they receive from their lips.

I.

The fact is first to be noted that there are *peculiar difficulties* in the way of maintaining a perfectly religious character in the family.

The importunate demands and the absorbing nature of household cares are familiar to every woman who has a home to superintend. These cares are apt to drive from the mind the thought of God, and to clog the channels through which spiritual motives and influences reach the heart. Unless a perpetual watch is kept up, they will leave the soul as blighted in its religious sensibilities and activities as is the field over which a frosty wind has been sweeping in its verdure and fruit. The independence which a man feels in the enclosure of his home may be fraught with danger. He is there responsible to no external authority. The eye of the public is absent, the judgments of the public are withdrawn. The necessity for self-control and for self-restraint is largely removed.

In this unhampered freedom in which a

man indulges when he closes his door upon the world without, he may be betrayed into intemperate practices even through his desire for ease and relaxation. The restiveness which leads him to shake off the yoke of care which has hung about his neck while engaged in the business of the day may go so far as to discard the yoke of duty which religion imposes upon him as the head of a family. The pent-up excitements engendered by intercourse with his fellow-men may at home relieve themselves in sourness of temper or in expressions of petulance. The chafed spirit may forget to wear before the gaze of children and domestics "the gentleness of Christ." The endearments with which an expectant household may be ready to greet the returning parent may be repelled as annoyances, and rebukes may chill the hearts which were longing for a caress. Weariness or indisposition may plead for the omission of family prayer and the other offices of domestic piety, until gradually every trace of the religious element may disappear from the family-life.

The old law which required the Israelite to write the precepts of the Lord upon the posts of his house and upon his gates (Deut. vi. 9) that he might be reminded of them as often as he crossed the threshold of his home is one which needs virtually to be observed by every Christian, for Satan may still insinuate himself into the domestic Eden and beguile both man and woman into forgetfulness of the commands of God.

II.

Household religion does not depend entirely upon positive methods and regulations. There is a form of it which lies back of these. It is *a pervading spirit* which gives a religious air or tone to the family-life. It is the result of a quiet—almost an unconscious—respect for the law of God as the principle which shapes in all its particulars the economy or *house-law* of the family.

When it is said (Gen. xviii. 19) of Abraham's household that they kept the "way of the Lord," it is meant that the whole manner of their domestic life evinced the fact that they were controlled by a regard for his will. The same thing ought still to be aimed at. Families are as capable of bearing and of exhibiting character as are individuals. They are corporate units and may be distinguished by specific marks. They have their different habits, pursuits, tastes and enjoyments. They are drawn together or repelled from one another by these predominating qualities. There are homes which the visitor at once feels to be religious homes, and in regard to which he says without any hesitation, "The Lord is in this place." There are other homes which are just as obviously irreligious. In a moment it is evident to the observer that God is in no way acknowledged in the constitution or the system of living of the family.

The character of a household will, of course, mainly depend upon those who are at the head of it and who enact and administer its laws, but to some extent it is due to the agency of each member of it. Now, clearly, the follower of Christ will be grossly forgetful of his duty everywhere to represent the properties of the "salt" or the "leaven" if he does not aim to give to the family to which he belongs a decidedly religious character. This result cannot be reached by a mere display of the symbols of religion, such as the presence of the Bible on a centre-table or the suspending of Scripture mottoes upon the walls, but by the effort of each member of the family himself to live under the influence of Christian motive and principle, and to incite and encourage all the other members to do the same. It is the brilliancy of the separate stars composing it which gives its brilliancy to a constellation. The Holy Spirit, developing those virtues of the heart and those graces of behavior and of manner of which he is the Author, in the person of each individual, will throw the combined lustre of these heaven-kindled lights into the character and the life of the whole family, and the result will be that the Christian home will stand among its godless neighbors an illumined object, like the dwellings of the Israelites in the midst of the darkened abodes of the Egyptians.

III.

It is too plain a proposition to call for argument that the maintenance of a religious character in the household *requires the observance of family worship.*

It is this which most sensibly enthrones God in a home, and by a literal expression of them gives form and tenacity to its religious sentiments. The gathering of a family together for the purpose of worshiping God is the most impressive act in which they can engage, and as suggestive or instructive as it is impressive. The echoes of the morning prayer or the Scripture lesson may linger in the mind of the hearer all through the day, and those of the evening's devotions may stir good thoughts upon the pillow or bring the atmosphere of heaven around the soul as sleep bears it into that mysterious state which is the image of death. The family is such a definite organism, its life is such a joint-stock of interest in which all the members are concerned, and its history necessarily contains so much of the experience of each separate constituent, that it would seem it must have some method or vehicle of proclaiming its religious faith and sentiment. Worship ought to flow through it as naturally as music flows through the pipes of an organ. A family which is never heard voicing its united thanksgivings to God or laying its wants and cares before his mercy-seat is an anomaly in the world.

The professor of religion cannot too soon admit to his mind the fact that God, in setting him at the head of a family, has set him there that he may be the priest of the household. It is his duty to see that God is worshiped in his home, and to seek to train there, as in a nursery, a band of worshipers who may in time perpetuate the hallowed ordinance in other homes. The penalty of a neglect of this duty will undoubtedly appear in the absence of all religious tendencies in the household. It is worthy of serious thought whether the drift of the youth of the present day away from the Church—a fact which is so much deplored—may not be owing to this cause, the omission of family worship, which is so largely prevalent in the homes of professed Christians.

In the case of most persons the difficulty of conducting this exercise is confessedly great—at least, in the first attempt. But the difficulty has been overcome in innumerable instances, and it should not be regarded is insurmountable in any. It will be materially diminished by an honest reflection upon the importance of the end to be attained, and by a simple trust in the aid promised by God to those who sacrifice their own will to his, and it will gradually vanish before repeated experiment. Family prayer, perfectly to fill its place, should be the free utterance of the person officiating in view of the varying phases of the family history; and where these are habitually reported to God—as they ought to be—by the Christian parent in the secrecy of the closet, it probably will not be hard to refer to them again in the devotions of the domestic circle. There may possibly be cases in which the ability to offer a prayer in public can never be acquired. In such cases, I would say, by all means let the person avail himself of the aid of such forms of prayer as may easily be obtained. These may to an imperfect extent give a voice to the family heart, and the use of their utterances is a thousand-fold better than a silent family altar.

IV.

Family religion must include, in some form, the *instruction of the young in religious matters*.

A pious parent, who feels that in being pious he is simply being what he ought to be, will feel, on the same grounds, that his children ought to be pious. And what he knows they ought to be he will try to make them. And the process by which a child is to be made anything is education or training. Certainly, he will not become a religious person unless he is taught what religion is and why he should be religious and how he is to be religious. To make no effort whatever in this direction is evidently to renounce all the obligations of parental duty. The heart would seem to be destitute of all natural as well as of all religious sensibility that could remain unmoved by the spectacle of a child in its helplessness appealing to a parent to give it the clue which shall safely guide it through the labyrinth of life upon which it has entered. And yet many parents excuse themselves from the attempt or satisfy themselves with delegating the task to servile hands.

This delinquency becomes the more flagrant when it occurs in the case of children dedicated, as they generally are by parents professing to be Christians, to God in baptism. This holy rite is a mockery if it does not amount to a solemn pledge made to God by the parents to give to their children the instruction and the culture needed to make them religious. No parent should dare to present a child for baptism unless he honestly and faithfully means to do this. It is superstition to seek baptism for a child in the belief that the mere application of water and the recital of a set of words will magically work the regeneration of its soul, and it is hypocrisy to profess to desire membership in the kingdom of God for a child while the parent has no other purpose than to bring it up for the world or for the devil.

The plea of incompetency is here again used to cover the neglect of parental duty. But surely any one who himself knows what it is to be a Christian can teach a child in many ways, indirect as well as direct, what it is to be one, or can in many particulars —and these perhaps the most essential —make him understand the difference between a man who is a Christian and one who is not. There are capacities—I might even call them instincts—in the nature of every child which point toward religion, and these may be fostered and cultivated. The nurture which is needed for this purpose is of the simplest sort. One does not require to be an adept in theology or a master in casuistry to call forth and to train such sentiments as conscientiousness, dependence upon God, reverence for his word and ordinances, complacency in virtue and aversion to vice, and delight in the evidences of divine loveliness contained in the character and the life of Christ. All of these are to be found waiting for development in a youthful mind.

Every parent professing to be a follower of Christ ought to be able to do these two things: first, so firmly to attach to himself the respect, the confidence and the affection of a child that nothing shall ever entirely obliterate them; and second, to fasten upon the child's mind the conviction that those qualities in the parent which have excited these feelings are due to his religion. When these things have been done, a volume of instruction will have been imparted which may be more potent than any formal homilies or any catechetical lessons. A mother beloved, and always appearing lovely through the charm which her piety gives her, is a living evangel perpetually preaching to the heart and the conscience of a child, and has been made in many instances the wisdom and the power of God unto the salvation of her child.

In teaching the young, the Bible is, of course, the source from which is to be drawn the knowledge to be communicated, and instruction is the imparting of this knowledge. The manner in which it is to be conveyed must be very much determined by the wise discretion of the parent. Aids in the formal part of this work are to be found in the elementary expositions of Scripture furnished by all the churches. There is, however, an informal way of giving instruction in religion which should never be divorced from the formal, and which may be even more effective than that. It consists more in *training* than in *teaching*—in showing a child how he is to apply the principles and actually to put in practice the precepts of the Bible. The same arts which are employed in teaching an infant to walk, and to walk in safe places, should be employed in teaching a young soul to take its steps and to choose its paths in the service of God.

V.

Religion in the family may be expected, on many accounts, to give a prominent place to *the observance of the Sabbath.*

The Sabbath and the family are kindred

institutions, derived from the same source—the ordination of God—and aiming at the same end, the rescuing of the soul from the wearying and the hardening influences of secular life. The answer to the Saviour's prayer in behalf of his exposed disciples, "I pray not that thou shouldest take them out of the world, but that thou shouldest keep them from the evil" (John xvii. 15), very largely comes through the channels of the home and the Sabbath. Through God's blessing the home may become the sanctuary within which the "evil" which everywhere tracks the steps of the follower of Christ while out in the world cannot intrude; and, in order to this, it needs to be shielded and barred by the hallowing influences of a weekly Sabbath against the assaults of "evil."

The benefits conferred upon a household by the day of sacred rest are so many and so great that the family which does not include in its house-law the fourth commandment, and which does not make provision for the keeping of it, would proclaim its ingratitude as loudly as it proclaims its irreverence; and the retribution for such a failure will probably appear in the loss of many of those special blessings, temporal as well as spiritual, which the household institution was intended to bestow.

The effort to make a family a Sabbath-keeping one will require much circumspection and study on the part of the heads of the household. Errors may be committed either on the side of over-strictness or on that of over-laxness. To strike the mean between the two—and in this case it is a "golden" one—is not easy. The first requisite is to familiarize a family with the idea that Sabbath-keeping is a law of the household. It should be made to take its place in the order of the family-life as naturally as the occupations of the weekdays take theirs.

The methods may vary more or less in their details in different households, but in all cases they must aim at distinguishing the Sabbath from other days, and distinguishing it by giving it a religious character. Household regulations should show this difference, and show it in a negative way, perhaps, as much as in a positive one—that is, as far as practicable, they should exclude from the Sabbath the employments of the weekday and the things which by association excite thought about these employments. The mind should be disencumbered of the burden of worldly care which the mere sight of the symbols of it lays upon it. On this account, if no other, the secular newspaper should be eschewed. It is in this way that the Sabbath most effectively verifies its name as a day of rest, for rest largely consists in the emancipation of the mind from a sense of the obligation to toil. Even the badges of servitude need to be withdrawn in order that it may feel truly free.

There is far more rest to be derived from laying this injunction—to use a legal phrase—upon the encroaching anxieties of worldly life than is to be found in the stupefaction of literal sleep. Rest, however, is not to be confounded with inaction. It consists, rather, in a change of action. The Sabbath, therefore, needs its occupations, and the difficulty in keeping it is to find these occupations and to give them a pleasant aspect. Among them, of course, there should be a due attention to the public worship of God. Where this cannot be rendered, as is sometimes the case in rural districts, there should be substituted family reading of the Scriptures, with singing and prayer. Families in which sacred music is cultivated will find themselves in possession of a decided advantage in the matter of Sabbath-keeping. Mere neighborly visiting and social festivity, simply because they are associated with the ordinary worldly life, ought to be suspended on the Sabbath, but visiting for purposes of mercy is a legitimate employment, and perhaps should receive more attention than it does. Weary hours might profitably be filled up in this way.

The quiet of the day of rest should evidently be improved by persons who have little leisure for religious reading during the week. And in the sweet reunion of the day large scope may be given to the interchange of home endearments. The domestic affections are sacred things, and the expression of them is not inconsistent with the hallowing of the Sabbath. The caress of a parent may give the best possible emphasis to the admonitions he has been addressing to a child. The day that most copiously sheds its dews upon the household heart and wakens into fresh vigor the spirit of family love is giving thereby not the least proof that it is itself the gift of Heaven and is fulfilling the end for which it was created. A father absent from his little flock—as many fathers are—during the week should feel that it is his privilege on the Sabbath to enjoy the blessing which God meant to bestow upon him in the companionship of that little flock. He should be glad himself, and should make all about him glad. There need be no restriction to the cheerfulness of the day except that which naturally arises from the reflection that the Sabbath is religious in its character, and must so recognize God as its Proprietor that even its gladness shall be sanctified by the spirit of worship."

VI.

All methods for maintaining or promoting piety in a family will fail, however, if they are not sustained by a *consistent, symmetrical and clearly-marked piety* in the heads of it.

From them the younger and inferior members will be continually getting their impression of the religion of Christ; and the follower of Christ needs to be a follower in whom there is no guile, and in regard to whose sincerity there can be no question within the precincts of a home. In the intimate associations of the household circle people come thoroughly to understand and to appreciate one another. Character cannot succeed in wearing a mask there. A parent who does not practice religion will frustrate the purpose of all his teachings. It is always to be borne in mind that children are not—generally, at least—disposed to be religious. The natural or "carnal mind" in them as in others is "enmity against God." It soon shows a repugnance to his law. The regimen it imposes upon them puts an annoying check upon the wild play of their desires and passions, and is a yoke which they are only too ready to elude where an occasion or a pretext is offered them. If any ground to distrust the claim of religion to be the rule and the exponent of goodness and the power which makes men good is presented to them in the conduct of those who profess to be its representatives, this aversion to it will gather strength as the flame does when fuel is added to it. In this matter the Saviour's saying (Matt. xii. 30) is emphatically true: "He that is not with me is *against* me, and he that gathereth not with me scattereth abroad."

Let the Christian parent never forget that the "demonstration" which the Holy Spirit will use in converting his children lies, to a great extent, in that which he is making of the purity and the excellence of godliness. They need to be won from dislike to the service of God by the sweet compulsion which forces them to love the parent or the kinsman whom religion has made worthy of their love. Everything in that parent or that kinsman which reveals a defect or a blemish in his character will be a weight in the scale against religion. It is the poor specimen of religion which professedly Christian men are exhibiting in their homes, probably, which more than anything else contributes to the readiness with which young people are taking in the current unbelief of the age or adopting the sophisms which beguile them into a worldly or a sensual life. The man who carries with him in his memory the image of a father or a mother in which every cherished feature is irradiated with the lustre of a genuine piety cannot easily become an infidel or sink so low in baseness as to call that a delusion or a falsehood which has enshrined such an image in his memory.

CHAPTER X.

RELIGION ALWAYS AND EVERYWHERE.

THE phrase "following Christ" obviously implies that a religious life is to be characterized by uniformity and stability. In the nature of it, it ought to be a continuous and an equable process. It is motion produced by the ceaseless attraction of a perpetually present object, not the fitful stir caused by occasional and irregular impulses. It is something by which the Christian is always and everywhere to be distinguished. In looking at it in various departments and under different relations, as we have been doing in the preceding pages, we have still considered it as one unbroken thread weaving itself into the warp of circumstance and maintaining its unity amidst all the facts with which it becomes intertwined. This comprehensive idea, containing, as it does, a summary of all the details of religious living, may suggest a few further reflections as a conclusion to this little treatise.

I.

It leads us, first, to the conclusion that the presence of the Christian spirit in a man is demonstrated by *the permanence of his convictions, sentiments and principles* rather than by what are called "frames of mind" or "excited emotions."

The awakening of any new affection in the soul if it be a wholesome one, or the apprehending of any new truth by it if it be a valuable one, will naturally be attended by a certain flush or exhilaration of feeling. This is to be expected in religion as well as in other phases of experience. No man can be conscious of the springing up in his heart of such an affection as love to God, or can seize with an appropriating faith such a truth as that "there is therefore, now, no condemnation to them which are in Christ Jesus" (Rom. viii. 1), without being by it transported into a distinct element of pleasure. A Christian, passing—as he sometimes does very sensibly—from darkness into light, will give evidence of the change as much by his joyful sensations as by his clear perceptions. Sometimes a new song is literally put into his mouth, and his rapture may be unspeakable.

Now, these first symptoms of a religious life are not to be taken as the abiding incidents of it. In ceasing to be new the affections and the beliefs which are coincident with the beginning of such a life cease to excite the subject with their original force and are entertained without any perceptible mental agitation. They show their presence by their fixedness rather than by their vehemence. The intense blaze into which a fire is fanned at the kindling of it dies down, but the fire fastened upon the ignited fuel burns on and emits its heat all the day. It is so in religion. It is a mistake to make elevated frames of feeling the main proof of spiritual life. This is to put a concomitant of religion for religion itself. There are times and places where the flame may be expected to blaze out, but the fire is the substantial thing which always and everywhere burns on with a steady glow. The Christian is known, and may know himself, better by those demonstrations which are uniform and regular than by those which are occasional and extreme. That "abiding" in Christ which the Saviour makes the test of the living disciple (John xv. 4) must consist in such exercises as are suitable to all occasions and all conditions. The "just" man, like his type the "shining light" (Prov. iv. 18), should at any hour of the day be found in his orbit, following with an unwavering step the path appointed for him by his great Lawgiver, Christ.

II.

The obligation to be religious always and everywhere implies that a Christian *should habitually be found in a state of preparation for all religious duties*, and for any particular religious duty which may suddenly arise.

The genuine artisan carries his wit and his skill with him, and is ready to respond to any call that may be made upon him without having to wait to sharpen his instruments and to quicken his faculties. So "the man of God" needs to be "thoroughly furnished unto all good works" (2 Tim. iii. 17). His soul should be always charged with the divine life, and not be required, like an exhausted battery, from time to time to be replenished with spiritual force. The follower of Christ who has to be waked up or recalled from some truant position every time his Master summons him to a service is certainly indulging himself in criminal drowsiness or presumption. The religious power or inspiration in the healthy Christian is something which is always as literally on hand and ready for use as is the natural power which leads to locomotion or the natural inspiration which prompts to gratitude or to indignation. Men do not have to prepare to walk, nor deliberately to kindle an emotion before they can thank a benefactor or rebuke a wrong-doer.

A consistent and continuous following of Christ will keep the professor of religion always in a state of preparation for any duty which his religion imposes upon him.

Temptation will never find him off his guard. An appeal to a religious motive will receive an instantaneous response. The call of Christ, "Go work to-day in my vineyard," at whatever moment it may come, will meet with the prompt and honest reply, "I go, sir." The wise virgins were provided with oil in their vessels and could keep their lamps always burning. There could be no jar upon their nerves, and there need be no flutter of mind or sinking of heart when the cry, "Behold, the bridegroom cometh!" smote upon their ears at the midnight hour.

The dependence upon special preparation as each step in the religious life is to be taken is significant of a lame and an uncomfortable walk. It assumes that religion is something extraordinary—something apart from common life; so that whenever an exhibition of it is required, there must be a shifting of the soul from one plane to another or a putting on of a new character for the occasion. Why should the man who is accustomed to pray for himself, and who knows how to tell his own wants to God, feel embarrassment, and perhaps give a refusal, when asked to pray for another? And why should so many professed Christians, when unexpectedly finding themselves present where the Lord's Supper is to be administered, decline to participate in it on the ground that they have had no opportunity for preparation? Does not such scrupulousness, while it seems to express reverence for the holy ordinance, just as plainly confess that in their ordinary state they are lacking in the faith and the love which believers ought always and everywhere to cherish toward their divine Redeemer?

A healthy condition of soul ought to have in it a sufficiency of warmth to make it able and ready at all times, without any special heating, to answer any demand for an expression of affection or devotion which Christ might present. It would carry the believer through all the extraordinary emergencies into which duty might call him as naturally as the waters of a full stream fill all the depressions and fit into all the windings of the channel through which it flows.

III.

Those peculiar privileges of the Christian life which are represented under the terms *peace* and *comfort* and *joy* are the product of that kind of religion which manifests itself always and everywhere.

The delightful sensations of health are not produced by tonics and stimulants. It is the combined play of all the organs of the body in the discharge of their regular functions which produces those sensations. The Christian who is not well poised and equable in his religious frames, who is always alternating between high states and low states of feeling, and who drops back into coldness as soon as the blast of some special excitement is turned off from his emotions, is not living in a healthy way. He will know little of true comfort in religion, or of genuine joy in believing, or of that peace of God which is able to keep his heart and mind through Christ Jesus. A settled faith in Christ, a fixed determination to follow him, a hearty and entire commitment of the soul to the method of salvation and the order of living proposed in the gospel, so that a suspicion as to one's being in Christ or a doubt as to the obligation of serving him in any particular would seem as anomalous as would a suspicion as to one's existence or a doubt as to obeying the laws of nature,—these things, which simply mean that a Christian is to be always and everywhere a Christian, are fundamental to all spiritual enjoyment. O professor of religion, in all positions, steadfastly, consistently, inflexibly, be what you profess to be, and religion will do for you all it promises to do.

One thing only is needed to secure the evenness of the Christian's walk, and that is always and everywhere to keep Christ in his eye as the object and the mark of his high calling. The light which gleams from the window of his home, kept constantly in view by the traveler groping his way toward it in the dark, is not only a guide to show him the right direction, but also an inspiration to help him over the casual obstructions of his path and a monitor to remind him of the illusions of the night by means of which he might be beguiled into a wrong road. The Christian who thus perpetually has Christ before him does not need special signals to assure him that he is in the way of heaven. He knows it just as he knows that he is always and everywhere following Christ.

IV.

Unhappily, professors of religion are not always *consistent and steadfast* in their following of Christ.

Disciples of Jesus may be found sleeping where he has commanded them to watch. Through heedlessness they may have allowed themselves to be "overtaken with a fault." Like Demas, they may have forsaken the post of duty through love of this present world. They may even, like Peter, apostatize so far as to deny their Lord and to associate themselves with his enemies.

Such defections on the part of Christians are, of course, at variance with all their obligations. They are criminal enough to make them fatal. And yet such breaches do not necessarily sever the connection between the soul and Christ. "If we believe not, yet he abideth faithful" (2 Tim. ii. 13). Always and everywhere present, he is still within the sight and the reach of his inconstant follower however far he may have wandered. The constancy and the unchangeableness of Jesus give hope to the backslider. He follows the straying sheep which has temporarily ceased to follow him. This fact keeps unbroken the connection between them. The storm has bruised the frail reed and bent it downward to the dust, but the sun looks upon it in its prostration and with the touch of its ray again lifts it into uprightness. So the touch of the Saviour's gracious hand is on the believer, even as he stands on the verge of forsaking his Master, so long as there is left in his heart a single yearning to prompt him to recoil from the final step, and, looking back to Jesus, to cry, "To whom shall I go? Thou hast the words of eternal life." Beneath all the accumulated guilt under which the faithless Peter lay Jesus could see the spark of love still glowing in his breast, and by the question, "Simon, son of Jonas, lovest thou me?" drew from him the response, "Lord, thou knowest all things, thou knowest that I love thee," by which his erring spirit swung back to the point of loyalty and devotion.

To the fallen Christian I would say, Still, in the depth of your sin and shame, follow Christ. Follow those craving impulses which are drawing you to him, and which forbid you to think that he has abandoned you. Follow them hopefully as the calls by which he is inviting you to return. They will bring you back to your right position in regard to him. They may even ensure the result that in the future you shall follow him with a more abiding steadfastness of purpose, and with a warmth of love quickened by the remembrance of your past errors.

V.

The habitual following of Christ is the condition of that *progress in religious character and activity* which every professor of religion is expected to make.

To follow is to copy or to imitate. To follow Christ is to become like Christ. This was one of the ends contemplated by God in the scheme of redemption: "For whom he did foreknow, he also did predestinate to be conformed to the image of his Son, that he might be the first-born among many brethren" (Rom. viii. 29). This purpose will undoubtedly be effected in the case of all who, with Christ as the ideal of the man of God in their eye, are striving to approach nearer and nearer to him in spiritual character and life. Such a following of Jesus will ensure the growth of the Christian, and will probably make it apparent to others, whether he sees and feels it or not. The infant grows to the stature of manhood without being able to detect the stages of the process through which he is passing.

The conditions of growth are to be observed; the manner of it is inscrutable. The child of God grows into the perfected man in the same way. As Christ is formed in him, he is conformed to Christ; and as he resembles Christ, he becomes the perfect man. The Holy Spirit, whose office it is to make men holy, accomplishes his work by bringing them more and more into assimilation to Christ. This he does by constantly keeping them under the influence of the direct vision of Christ: "We all, with open face, beholding as in a glass the glory of the Lord, are changed into the same image, from glory to glory, even as by the Spirit of the Lord" (2 Cor. iii. 18). Always and everywhere following Christ, the believer may rest in the assurance that God is finishing his work in his soul and carrying him along, stage after stage, in that process of growth by which he is to be presented faultless and complete in Christ Jesus.

VI.

As following Christ aims, as its present result, at making the believer like Christ, so, as its ultimate result, it aims at bringing the believer into *personal* association with Christ.

"Father, I will that they also whom thou hast given me, **be with me**, where I am," was the last prayer offered by Jesus for his disciples on earth (John xvii. 24). To be present with the Lord, St. Paul tells us, is coincident with being absent from the body. The following of Christ ends at death in an introduction to the presence of Christ. The process has this consummation infallibly guaranteed to it, and the believer, in pursuing it, is warranted in encouraging himself with the expectation of this glorious issue. The follower of Christ ought, therefore, in consistency, to include this residence with his Lord in his view of the future, and to be accustomed to solace himself amidst the labors and hardships of his earthly walk with the anticipation of heaven.

This hope will often be the only anchor which can keep his soul steadfast in the storms of life. This is not saying that it is required of the Christian that he should desire to die. This would be to act insanely. It would be to deny his nature and really to long to extinguish the being to which, both by his own instincts and by the will of his Maker, he is bidden to cling. It is not the spirit of the mystic buried, in a mistaken pursuit of holiness, in a monastic prison or desert, and dreaming of the contents of a paradise which in his imagination floats above him, that he is to exhibit. But, just as he knows that this life is to have an end, it is his privilege to look beyond that end and to construe its ending into the inception of a higher state of being, and to balance against the ills of time and the painful cost of fidelity to God now the rest and the blessedness which are pledged to those who are faithful unto the end in following Christ.

It is the man who most truly values and uses this life as a period of service for Christ who is most truly showing his fitness for the inheritance and the crown which Christ will award to his loyal followers. But there may be an aspiration in the Christian's soul reaching heavenward all the while that the natural love of life is asserting itself in that soul. It is the aspiration which is always aiming at something better beyond which nerves and sustains the spirit in the whole struggle of life. The child of God cannot be content with present attainments, with present joys, but must be conscious of an aspiration which looks beyond these to the glory which is to be revealed. He is saved by the hope which forecasts the being with Christ as well as by the faith which relies upon Christ, for the former is the product of the latter.

It is not impatience under the present allotments of Providence, not the chafing of the soul at the burdens and restraints with which it is environed, not the passionate beating of the imprisoned breast against the bars of its cage, which denote the temper of the Christian, but it is the quiet waiting of the watcher who during the night-hours encourages himself with the prospect of the daybreak, and the cheerful ongoing of the pilgrim pressing through the rigors of the wilderness to the Canaan beyond the flood.

Follower of Christ, familiarize your mind with the thought that soon and for ever you are to be with the Lord. Set over against all the attractions of this life the attractions of the life which is to come. Assert your kinship with God by daring to say, "I shall be satisfied when I awake in thy likeness." This anticipation, this aspiration, always and everywhere kept in your mind, will loosen your attachment to this world, will chasten your ardor in the pursuit of its joys, will lighten the pressure of its momentary sufferings, and will enable you, while sharing in the apostle's blessed assurance, "Now are we the sons of God," to share also in his exulting hope for the future: "It doth not yet appear what we shall be, but we know that when he shall appear, we shall be like him, for we shall see him as he is."

CHAPTER XI.

CONCLUSION.

IT may be well, in order to give practical point and direction to the didactic discussions contained in the previous chapters, to sum them up in a series of resolutions embodying—at least, partially—the conclusions to which we have been brought. It is the resolution to perform a duty which gives effect to a conviction of duty. The man who, by becoming a church-member, has acknowledged his obligation to lead a religious life, and by that solemn act has engaged to lead such a life, should deliberately shape his convictions into resolutions, with the sincere determination to carry them into practice. To aid him in this work, the following schedule is appended to this treatise.

I.

I am resolved, as a member of that distinct body of Christ's followers to which I have attached myself, constantly to bear in mind the responsibilities which belong to my corporate character, and in all circumstances to conduct myself as a personal representative of that religion which the Church of Christ was appointed to illustrate to the world.

II.

I am resolved to make the Bible my lifelong study, and to seek, through the blessing of the Holy Spirit upon my effort, to grow more and more in the knowledge of divine truth, that I may live more and more under the power of it.

III.

I am resolved always to be present at the house of God at the stated times of public worship, unless the providence of God should by some clear obstruction prevent my attendance.

IV.

I am resolved habitually to practice secret prayer, and to accustom myself to think of God and to commune with him during the occupations of the day.

V.

I am resolved to make my family religious as well as myself, and to this end to see that they keep holy the Sabbath-day, to teach them to become worshipers of God by leading them to the place of public worship and by conducting worship with them at home, and to inculcate upon them the idea that the law of the household is the law of the Lord.

VI.

I am resolved to keep Christ in my view as the model whom I am to follow, and not the imperfect types of piety which I may see in the professed Christians around me.

VII.

I am resolved to watch against my peculiar infirmities and perseveringly to endeavor to subdue the faults to which I am liable.

VIII.

I am resolved to be scrupulously honest and truthful in all my dealings with my fellow-men.

IX.

I am resolved to cultivate charitable feelings toward all my fellow-members of the church, to yield respect to the counsels of its officers, and to show such consideration for my pastor as to inform him of any occasion for his services which may occur, through sickness or otherwise, in my family or my neighborhood.

X.

I am resolved, while acting with kindness and courtesy toward all, to abstain from such associations, amusements and places of resort as might be detrimental to my own spiritual good or expose me to the charge of giving countenance to the enemies of Christ.

XI.

I am resolved to do my part according to my ability in bearing the burdens and sustaining the benevolent enterprises of the Church.

XII.

I am resolved to keep myself informed in regard to the work of the Church and the progress of Christ's kingdom in the world, and for this purpose to provide myself and my family, where this is possible, with some religious periodical.

XIII.

I am resolved, in humble dependence upon Christ's help, to maintain my loyalty to him under all the temptations which may come to me through the allurements or the oppositions of the world, or through the successes or the reverses which may be included in my lot in life.

XIV.

I am resolved to place my devotion to my worldly business under such restrictions that it shall never interfere with the duties which I owe to God as a Christian and as a church-member.

XV.

I am resolved to remember that as a child of God I am also his heir, destined to inherit a heavenly home which I may at any moment be called upon to enter, and to use this expectation and this hope as a constant means of checking an inordinate attachment to the present world and of keeping myself in a state of readiness for my departure from it, endeavoring, in imitation of the apostle's faith, to say, "To me to live is Christ, and to die is gain" (Phil. i. 21).

THE END.

www.ingramcontent.com/pod-product-compliance
Lightning Source LLC
Chambersburg PA
CBHW021821230426
43669CB00008B/823